SWAG
101

SWAG 101

Invisible Mechanics, Perfect Collisions and .400 Hitters

ROB CREWS

iUniverse LLC
Bloomington

SWAG 101
Invisible Mechanics, Perfect Collisions and .400 Hitters

iUniverse books may be ordered through booksellers or by contacting:

iUniverse LLC
1663 Liberty Drive
Bloomington, IN 47403
www.iuniverse.com
1-800-Authors (1-800-288-4677)

ISBN: 978-1-4917-1157-6 (sc)
ISBN: 978-1-4917-1158-3 (e)

Printed in the United States of America.

iUniverse rev. date: 10/11/2013

This book is dedicated to Mr. Burt Kaufman of Eastchester, New York—a man who gave my grandmother an opportunity in spite of racial segregation even before civil rights. He remains a loyal family friend and his work ethic, moral fabric, and humility has inspired me to great lengths.

SWAG 101 is also dedicated to my students because everything I am teaching is what I have learned from you.

Romans 12:2

"And be not conformed to this world: but be ye transformed by the renewing of your mind, that ye may prove what is that good, and acceptable, and perfect, will of God." The Holy Bible, King James Version

INTRODUCTION

I honestly thought the first book would be the last. However, my readers have seduced me into writing what now has become a series of books. My personal journal of thoughts on subjects related to player development. I sat on this book for more than year, coming up with all sorts of excuses as to why I should delay its release. I felt like it was too deep and people wouldn't understand my weirdness. I would jokingly say to people, "They're either gonna say I'm crazy or a genius." I wonder if there's a difference . . .

The books are my way of documenting my thoughts, research, and experience regarding the proper development of athletes with a special emphasis on hitting. As you can sense, development, techniques, and the way in which athletes learn are constantly evolving. The Complete Game Book Series is the best way for me to archive, organize, and deliver information to my readers. Since the trajectory of learning has changed, the trajectory of teaching must change as well. There is a real need for innovation in teaching techniques. Therefore, I am growing along with my students. It seems as though every few months we get a break-through of some sort in terms of teaching and learning. So here we go . . .

SWAG 101—the paradox. The "101" signifies that SWAG can actually be taught—but can it really? Maybe not. If SWAG is simply defined as an air of confidence, then it is my understanding that confident is not something one does—it is something one is. And someone cannot "act" confident because if you have to convince yourself, then you are deceiving yourself. Is SWAG 101 a play on words?

Let me ask you a question: I know that you can be a great athlete and lack SWAG, but "Can an athlete who is less than elite have SWAG?" I don't think so. I mean people with an authentic swag can smell a phony—the ones who try way too hard. But we like that word—SWAG. It has a certain ring to it. So we throw that word around like love or hate—or awesome. SWAG has become somewhat of a semantic satiation. Now everyone's is walking around talking about, "I got so much SWAG." Who started that anyway? I will blame rappers for making it popular and the rest of us for adapting it.

Now the perfect collision as you will read later, only occurs when everything mentally, visually, and physically in the hitting process happens without flaw, resulting in a hard hit ball with the perfect amount of trajectory and back spin that leaves people in awe, even you—the hitter. But preparation is the key. Preparation is the never-ending quest to rehearse and perfect those parts of the process that will ultimately lead to success. In this case, the catch, the pitch, the swing, the game—the PERFECT COLLISION! SWAG 101, is all about how we prepare or train as athletes. Not really about right or wrong but taking a look at some different perspectives.

Sometimes I find myself attempting to teach people to be confident. As a coach, its part of my job to give my students a sense of confidence. The rest is really up to the individual player. This whole concept of bulletproof confidence—what is that? Is it even possible, or some sort of lie? I'm not sure. I guess it is a matter of how much I can convince myself how much badassness I possess. Or how much of a BA I want to be. But nevertheless there is something about swag that makes you wonder. In a world of opposites I often wonder if the person with the most swag has the deepest fear of failure. In my own swag lies the possibility of not living up to what I am projecting. And that fact alone can be the origin of my fears. So is confidence merely a shell wrapped around your deepest fears? The fear of possibly not being able to perform or live up to expectations. It's weird how I can admire that person who embraces their fears. Accepts them—sort of like a baby. *"I am afraid of the dark."* or, *"I am afraid of heights and I don't care who knows. Now watch me cry."* Since we're not babies, we can't cry although the honesty would be liberating. Somewhere along the line we have learned not to cry, not to be weak. So there's No Crying in Baseball— at least not on the outside. That would be too much transparency, but much easier than the stress or pressure of having to appear to be bulletproof. I have seen softball players well into womanhood cry (on the field), but it was a good cry or should I say a justifiable weep. Now I am not saying go out and throw your helmet because you sucked today. But I am encouraging you to understand the emotions you feel and learn what to do with them or better yet where to put them. And after competitive redemption has had her way, you can access those emotions later and deal with them. Perhaps it takes more guts to admit your shortcomings than to smear false confidence all over them. I remember my Mother sending me upstairs into the darkest parts of the house to get a diaper for my younger sister. I was petrified of the dark but I would have to conjure up the courage, stick my chest out (literally), go upstairs and face it.

Good athletes can't afford to allow their competition to know they have a weakness. And the great ones don't even allow their teammates to know, unless it's in private. Some of us won't even admit our weaknesses to our own selves. There's a word for that—denial, which can be the root of a lot of personal and athletic shortcomings. However, the seasoned, veteran athlete will take responsibility and accountability and share his issues with an understanding coach or mentor.

Giant Athletes, much like tall buildings have this hidden foundation that we never see. But we know the taller the structure, the deeper the foundation. Could it be that the confident ones have this deep-rooted issue? This issue that goes deeper than we can see or even imagine and is often camouflaged in humor, loudness, false confidence, arrogance, or contempt. And at the high school, college, and professional levels, many athletes hide out in the caves of drug/alcohol use, partying, reckless intimacy, and other social deviant behaviors (and yes weed is an illegal drug and beer is alcohol). You can't really talk about it and you better not ever even think of showing it. You express it in your own ways. You find people who are just like you and create this world of your own. Go to the same places and eat the same foods and even dress the same. Play the same game? And in that self-made pseudo-world it seems as though everything is better. You can escape true reality by creating your own personal reality. Now reality has become whatever you need it to be—or whatever you want it to be. And then one day your make-believe world spits you out and you have to deal with true reality. Fear overcomes you because you cannot separate what is real from what is not. Then that question comes up—Now what? That haunting reality check type of question. NOW WHAT?

I do believe its possible to find strength in your own weakness. Hope in your own despair—confidence in your own fears. In my own personal pursuit of finding better ways to help my athletes to achieve that bulletproof confidence necessary to achieve their goals, I am learning how deep the mind can go. And for this reason, good hitting will never be a swing, but always a mindset. We see the swing on the physical plane but there are invisible mechanics that occur in which we will never see. It is possible to have an abundance of the necessary swagger for projecting successful body language, and lack or lose access to the skill set necessary for attaining that level of success you once knew or perhaps will never know. It happens all the time. Here in the 21st Century, we are seeing the decline in skills of a lot of athletes. They reach their prime, and with their decline, the next generation of superstars will emerge. And although they may still have the swag, the physical prowess that supported the swag is slowly fading. I have also seen Manny Ramirez in his prime, walk back to the dugout after a strikeout, like he just hit a grand slam. I believe he knows that he is not the strikeout for that is temporary and not permanent. Some might interpret it as he doesn't care, but I would say they're right, he doesn't care about what already happened but he is more concerned about what he will make happen next! In fact, it is safe to say he will be successful in his next opportunity just because he needs to redeem himself from the past.

So back to the perfect collision—what is that? The perfect collision begins first with the ability to access and replicate a perfect thought process. This perfect thought process varies from hitter to hitter but always originates beneath the surface—then the manifestations of the hitter's thought process surfaces to where we can see it and feel it. I believe in the possibility of the perfect collision. I believe that when everything happens perfectly—that is on time, with the right angle, and great extension, hitters can experience a sort of NIRVANA or the Perfect Collision.

Somewhere along this road to wherever we are going as athletes, many of us have been deceived. We have been duped into believing that confidence is this or confidence is that, only to find out that it really isn't. I believe that one of the biggest deceptions known to athletes is the true definition of confidence. I often hear the term bulletproof confidence thrown around and sports psychologists assisting athletes in the development of a false sense of confidence and I am wondering if it can even be taught—in a classroom. If you have not already seen the movie Green Lantern, it is a must see for every athlete. While it wasn't really a thriller on the excitement side, it was rather insightful and motivating if you like great stories and compelling content.

The movie really made me think about confidence and fear, the root of it all. The movie forced me to begin to deal with the fact that confidence has one enemy in that of fear. The creators of comic books have a unique gift for bringing our personal demons into life forms portrayed as villains and eventually conquered by super heroes. Now there are tons of definitions for fear. I looked up many of them. One thing we know is that fear is an emotion or has its root in our emotions. We also, know that fear is almost always a mere perception, whether a threat is real or not. And the problem with perceptions is that they are almost always personal, and have something to do with our minds, our past experiences, memories, or what we have been taught. Some basketball players may fear going to their left while some hitters may fear the change-up. Some people may fear public speaking, spiders, heights, or the dark. In the case of the Green Lantern Movie, the Green Lantern Core, a team of chosen, elite, defenders of the universe, were afraid to admit they were afraid. Hmmmm.

The story is about a guy named Hal Jordan, the first human to be chosen to wear "the ring" and become apart of the Green Lantern Core. In order to be chosen to be a member of the core, "one must be without fear." The Core's common enemy is Parallax, an evil villain who possesses the yellow power of fear and grows more powerful with each encounter, feeding on the fear of each victim.

Hal eventually masters the knowledge of how to harness the green power of his own Will, transforming his thoughts into reality by learning to focus his mind. He realized the ring's limits are only what he can imagine. Of course fear and doubt creeps in, and Hal is told, "The ring chose you, it would not have done so if it hadn't seen something in you, something you yourself don't yet see." I wonder how many athletes have been chosen and are competing at a level that is presently above them only to eventually grow into it. Sometimes we need someone to believe in us, even when we don't believe in ourselves—ESPECIALLY when we don't believe in ourselves. But at some point we do have to actually believe in ourselves. Who is that person or people in your life?

The Green Lantern movie gives us jewels of wisdom such as, "Fear is the enemy of Will. Will is what makes you take action. Fear is what stops you, and makes you weak. When you are afraid you can't act. When you can't act, you can't defend. When you can't defend, you die." So basically the movie reminds us that fear cripples and disables the very process necessary for success.

After being discriminated against for being a mere human, Hal then goes on an unassisted quest to destroy Parallax and save the planet Earth. Proving that the human will is stronger than fear. In SWAG 101, we will identify specific areas of performance governed by the human will and how you as an athlete can access and control it to aid in your success.

In the world of sports performance, athletes operate on three very fundamental levels. (1) The law of the land or physics, (2) the law of our body or kinetics, and finally (3) the law of our minds.

The law of the land can never really change since elements such as atoms, gravity, and all other quantum electrodynamics are what they are—constant. Changes that occur on that level cannot be perceived on our human level. With proper swing movements and body positioning we can work with the laws of the land and not against them. For example, a hitter with higher hands in the setup works with gravity (bat swings itself) in their path to the ball, while lower hands require more (up hill) work as we go against gravity.

The law of our body has certain limitations such as genetics and what physical condition we're in. The body can change based upon our work/rest ethic, diet, and whether or not we workout properly. The tempo, direction, and sequence of movement in a particular task are the keys to maximizing speed, strength, rhythm, and balance. If one part of the kinematic sequence is off, it can change the result dramatically. For example, we know that in a proper kinematic sequence, power in a swing or throw is generated from the ground up through the feet into the hands or bat. But if the feet are not positioned properly that flow of energy or power will not be transferred to the bat or arm for power.

Our brains, when stretched is constantly learning and adapting. Therefore the Law of the Mind is limitless. It is tied into something with infinite possibilities. Our faith, belief-system, imagination, focus, confidence, testicular fortitude, clarity of thought, and vision are key here. These are all invisible mechanics or something I often refer to as an Athletic Operating System (AOS). There are so many levels of consciousness the mind can attain. Some of us, with equal skill-sets and better results, are simply operating on "another level," in our minds. And that level, while having it's origin and potential in our mind and imagination, manifests itself in our reality. It is basically the difference between Windows 98 or the latest version of Windows. If I can point out how much belief systems play a part in a player's success, I can articulate in one sentence. "If a player believes that a certain coach cannot help him, he is right and should go find someone he believes can help him." That is how important faith and believing are and it is a big part of the AOS.

Q: Well coach. How do I get to the elite level? I swing everyday. I go to my personal trainer. I do motion analysis on the video camera. I have all these new hitting gadgets and fancy batting tees. I'm on this really good team now. What's next?

A: This is where people get stuck. There is a wall blocking their progress and they are spending so much time trying to get over it or under it. On the other hand, the people on the other side of the wall have changed their perception of the wall and walked right through it—sort of like Casper. Take for instance Michael Jordan defying gravity with his hang time. This is an example of how the law of your Mind can take the other Laws, which have specific limitations, far beyond their boundaries. And because we cannot see the Mind, we try to change the things we can actually see— such as the swing. Ever thought of changing your mind? Well, in order for mind-transformation to occur, there must be an exchange of thoughts and feelings from student to teacher to student. I am finding that when I ask the students certain questions, the information I receive helps me to better help them. Knowing and understanding how students think is the only way to really help them. Simply presenting your hitting model more than likely conflicts with what they are thinking. Find out what they are thinking by learning from them first, and then you can know exactly what to present and how to present it.

There is an interconnectivity of Mind and Body that cannot be ignored. Mind Training must come first or be taught along with body control or mechanics. If we continue to teach them separately our players will not develop and mature properly as they move on to higher levels of competition. In order to realize success, we have to fuse Mind and Body principles together in our respective teaching models.

Q: Why did you decide to write a book?

A: I have always been a writer. Writing is one of my passions. One of the main reasons I decided to write books on performance is because when I work with my athletes, I don't always have the time to spend on the mental game that I would like. My writing gives me a chance to speak to them in their solitude and connect with their mind. The athletes can read it and take it all in at their own pace. They can read and re-read certain parts that are special to them as it is another powerful form of communication.

ROB CREWS

Q: How did you get into softball?

A: The truth is I didn't get into softball. Softball got into me. I was doing the same thing I am doing now in baseball first. In fact, I still work with baseball players. However, back in the late 90's most baseball instructors didn't want to work with girls and most softball coaches (at least the ones here on the east coast) didn't believe the baseball swing could be the same as the softball swing. Personally, I could not see why it would be different unless you were sexist in your thinking and felt like girls were physically unable to swing correctly. I believe the softball swing, emerged due to the false pretense that girls can't do it right and must be taught the girl way. So I had a choice to make. I could either follow the pack or stick to what I truly believed. And I truly believed in my heart of hearts that I could teach girls the right way to swing a bat however controversial the "baseball swing" was back then, my advantage was that I wasn't seeking the approval of the softball world. I was already successful in the baseball world. It seems that in softball everyone wants to agree. I think the differences and varieties are what make teaching and learning great, especially if what you're teaching works. Who cares if it's different?

Anyway, there were these three Dads here in southern Westchester County (NY), former college and pro baseball players, and coaching their daughters on a team called the Hudson River Bandits. It was probably the first and last time we (in Westchester) have seen a team where the dads actually knew what they were doing. They were the only ones crazy enough to let a baseball guy teach a baseball swing to their softball team back then. Remember that on the East Coast, people were strict about this baseball versus softball swing thing. All the games were 1 or 2 nothing. 13 or 15 strikeouts. It was crazy. Boring is what it was. I realized why they called it fastPITCH because it was all about the pitcher. Anyway, this team of 10 and 12 year olds would come in to hit twice per week for 2 hours a clip. They were all focused—something you don't see much of nowadays. This team went down to nationals and placed 2nd which didn't happen with northeast teams at all. But apparently they hit the ball.

There were a lot of very good players that would emerge from this group but 2 in particular really put softball on the map for our area. Their parents were crazy enough and committed enough to venture out to the world of competitive softball, which could only be found in other parts of New York or out of state. The best softball is still found in other parts of New York or out of state to this day—mainly because the mindset is different in those places. This is a very privileged area here in Westchester. So you kind of have to get out of the mindset in order to better appreciate the worldview. We truly are products of our own environment but we don't have to accept it. Anyway it was in far away places where they would test their skills against the best talent in the country. During which time I was still training them, but had no idea the level of success they were realizing. In fact, both Ali and Maddy would go on to be a big part of the VA Shamrocks offense in their 2005 ASA national title.

Ali Gardiner and Maddy Coon's success really inspired my love for softball. It was their success that caused everyone to take notice to what was going on in the basement of a small indoor training center called Frozen Ropes in southern New York. And although both of them have gone on to do great things in and out of the world of softball, the thing I brag the most about is the extraordinary women they have become today—off the field.

Q: Tell us about your Youth?

A: Growing up in New Rochelle NY, the block seemed so big. When I drive through my old block today it seems so small. I remember barely being able to hit a home run onto the roof of the building across the street. Today those would be routine pop ups.

Yeah, May Street was known as the baseball block. In my neighborhood, if you were a kid, and you wanted to come outside and play, you had no choice because that is all we played. Flipping baseball cards and chewing on huge wads of bubble gum was our pastime. Nobody could afford to actually go away on vacation. Our definition of vacation was no school. Getting on a plane just didn't happen and actually going somewhere was a rarity.

I remember the year I was selected for the Babe Ruth All-Star team and didn't want to play. Quite frankly, the baseball in my neighborhood was 10 times better. My father made me go back down to the field and get back on the team. I understood why he did it later on, but at the time it was like why play with the scrubs with the politics of league play when I could play against real baseball players in my own neighborhood.

Q: What do you think is the biggest misconception about you and what you do?

ROB CREWS

A: That was a good question. What's funny is that when people ask me what I do, I often don't know what to say.

I think there are more than one misconception about what I do and me. First, so many people think that I work exclusively with the "good players" or the "good teams" when in fact, I will train anyone who wants to learn. In fact, I would rather take the player that everyone has given up on and turn that player around. I love working with that borderline athlete that is so close but yet so far away from realizing their true potential. Many of those "good teams and players" I work with were something else before you heard of them. Just ask them.

Second misconception is that I only teach hitting. So many people don't know that I work with infielders and outfielders in addition to hitting. I have retired from softball pitching but I still train baseball pitchers. I teach movement. I think all master teachers are gifted in the area of discerning movement. It doesn't matter who is moving. It could be a tennis player. If you know what it is supposed to look like, you can figure out how to articulate it. That is the real gift—the communication of the knowledge.

The third one probably should be number one is that I don't teach a swing. There is a misunderstanding that I teach the rob crews swing. But if you go west or even south you will see that is just the way a lot of hitters have been taught to hit. It is most certainly not the rob crews swing. I didn't come up with a swing. That is just absurd. In fact, the very thing that separates my hitters from a lot of other hitters is totally invisible—it is mental and visual. So people can duplicate the swing but they can't duplicate those hidden things that just don't show up on video analysis software but are precisely the cause of the things that do show up in the results. I call these Invisible Mechanics. At the more elite levels of hitting, it would be egotistical for me to need to make someone hit the way I think they should. Instead, I need to be more concerned with learning from them, so I can understand how they already hit or how they need to hit. This information is usually buried in layers somewhere near a hitter's core—the heart.

Teaching at this level for a hitting coach is different. We are learning from hitters, rather than telling them what we think they need to know. The only box a hitter should be in is the batter's box—not my box—certainly not the box that we hitting coaches like to teach in. There are far too many ways a hitter can be successful. It cannot possibly be that my way is one size fits all. Instead, hitting and swings are like fingerprints and unique to the hitter. The more time I spend with a hitter, the easier to crack that particular hitter's code. And then once the code is cracked, it can mysteriously change again. I always tell my students the best hitting coach you'll ever have is you. Some hitters just need to know how to figure themselves out. The exchange of knowledge and feedback mixed with experimentation is necessary and ongoing in most cases. I find that most coaches' mediocrity stems from their unwillingness to experiment.

It is the invisible things that a hitter does that I can only find out about through engaging the student in a conversation—allowing them to feel comfortable enough with me and share their feelings and thoughts regarding the process. In this place, I can really get a sense of what they believe and better understand what they are trying to accomplish. From here we move closer to the Perfection Collision.

So I need to be able to answer these questions:

What are you thinking about?
What are you looking for?
What are you looking at?

And so many others. Its almost as though I need to interview them to find out where they are? Because without this foreknowledge how can I really help them?

If you have just recently purchased a new cell phone you will have noticed that the contents of the box will include the following:

Phone
Battery/Cover
Charger
Earpiece
Quick instruction guide
Manual

It's funny how the manufacturers know we most certainly will not read the full manual so they include a short version of the manual. And of course many of us don't even read that. A month after you receive the phone, after never acknowledging the manual, we realize that our phones can do more than we thought. Three months later, we realize that our phones can do even more amazing things. So my point is, imagine if we would have read the manual before we began to use the phone? We would have known from the beginning all of the 'secret powers' of our mobile devices and been closer to expert level in it's operation.

Now my question to every coach and athlete is, imagine if we took the time to learn the manual of our bodies? There are many coaches and athletes out there teaching and competing without a clue as to how the body functions faster, stronger, and more efficiently. Many athletes are merely learning as they go along—trial and error. Sort of like the cell phone user. Believe it or not, my best hitters and my best students are my smartest students. They know more about a swing than many of the team coaches. They are students of their bodies and the game. You better believe a NASCAR driver knows how to take his own car apart, and put it back together again. And so should a hitter their bodies, it's movement, sequences, and tempos. She should know how the mind-brain activity affects the sequences, tempos, and direction in which the body moves. He should also know how the eyes fit into that process of recognition and reaction. Learning how to fuse all these factors together develops one's individual template for perfection. The higher the level you are striving for, the more you need to know. So SWAG 101 is intended to give you the manual—perhaps not the entire manual, but a pretty good chunk of it.

As an instructor-teacher I try to give my students a piece of the manual every time we meet. Knowing full well that the only way they can truly be successful at the higher levels of competition is to literally become their own coach just as a NASCAR driver has to become her own mechanic. Every player doesn't totally evolve into some master hitter overnight but everyone grows at his own rate. For some it may take 8 months and for others, 2 years. How quickly athlete's retain growth depends on a number of variables ranging from genetics to environment to work ethic. If you ever speak to professional athletes they will tell you that have actually learned things about themselves in professional experience they never knew at the amateur level. And many of them were pretty darn good as amateurs.

CHAPTER 1

Training Styles, Techniques & Modalities

"I'll teach it, if you learn it."—Rob Crews

SEEING VS. FEELING

Is seeing always believing? I am not so sure this premise is a premise when it comes to swing analysis. Since about 70 percent of children have a primary learning modality of FEEL and not VISUAL, why would this method of teaching be so important? I do believe it is necessary for a player who falls into that less than 30 percentile. But what percent of the remaining 70 percent is audio or visual? Coaches stand to benefit more from this video software than most players do. I have found that while so many coaches are using video analysis software, many don't know what they are looking for.

Don't get me wrong—I love technology. If you ask anyone who knows me, they will tell you that I have every gadget known to man. If you are using software programs, or any tools that assist with developing hitters, be sure you know what your team or the player's primary learning modality is. Start out by determining what their modality is.

DETERMINING LEARNING MODALITY

I can usually determine what an athlete's learning modality is by having a conversation with them. Sometimes I can find it by seeing how they respond to feel drills. In teaching, I always teach in three modalities. I say it (audio), demonstrate it (visual), and then I give the players a drill(s) (kinetic/feel). I really believe that because I can demonstrate everything I teach, this makes me more effective in getting my students to understand by seeing. Here is where video would come into play. If you have video footage of players who are performing the task correctly, then it is worth showing video. Once you have become better acquainted with your hitters, you can group them together by modality and give players specific drills that actually match their learning modality.

The Learning Styles Inventory (Brown, J. F.; Cooper, R. M. 1976) was used to assess the students. The Learning Styles Inventory (LSI) is the only modality inventory that measures math-learning styles. The LSI has nine categories, which are:

TEACHING BY MODALITY

Visual Language—you learn language skills best by sight and reading
Visual Numerical—you do better with numbers when see them written
Auditory Language—you learn best by listening
Auditory Numerical—you learn best with numbers when you can hear them
Tactile Concrete—you are a builder and learn best when you can touch what you are studying
Social Individual—you prefer to work on your own
Social Group—you learn best by interacting in groups
Oral Expressiveness—how well you express yourself when you verbally
Written Expressiveness—how well you express yourself in writing

Having this sort of knowledge gives you a tremendous amount of effectiveness in teaching, training, and coaching. Instead of forcing every student to learn in the same way, we can now pinpoint each student's specific learning preference and design our drills and teaching methods accordingly. You will find that so many hitters are unique in how they absorb information but many teachers have only mastered or are comfortable coaching one way. Then we blame the student for not being able to learn it, but we (as teachers) really failed to connect with them. I have been guilty of that in the past. But more recently, I have been able to customize my approach to match each athlete's strengths in learning. For example, I have learned to allow my athletes to do things that don't exactly fit what I believe. Since it works for the athlete and they are realizing success in a certain comfort level, we sync some things they like to do with some new things. People adapt better this way. I have even learned how to pair the athletes that are similar and assign certain drills to match their preferences.

PLAYER TYPES V.I.P.

The Visualizer—These are the athletes who listen and translate the words presented into pictures. The Visualizer displays the words as pictures onto their mental TV screens. Some athletes display what they've absorbed in HD quality while others in black and white. Sometimes you can be talking to 10 people and only 3 are actually listening and 1 person gets it. For example, you can give your team post-game instructions on where and what time dinner is and what time curfew is and what time to be ready for breakfast. And then immediately after your speech, there will always be that player or players who will ask another teammate, *"Wait, what are we doing?"*

Those are your players who need you to write it down for them. Imagine when you tell them adjust their stride length or extend through the ball, et cetera.

The Intellectual—This is the athlete who processes everything intellectually. He really has to understand it. She would never drive a car unless she knew how it worked from tires to steering wheels. This is why hitting coaches who don't know what they're doing can't help certain hitters. The intellectual hitter will tend to over analyze everything—often times their intelligence becomes the very thing hindering them. As coaches, we need to give these players something to think about (a focal point) in order to distract them from their own selves.

The Physical One—This is the athlete who does it, feels it, and masters it—in like 5 minutes. There aren't that many players like this, but they are a pleasure to coach.

The Beast—The Beast is a combination of all three. She is the intellectual visualizer with incredible physical body and muscle control in the areas of tempo, direction, and sequence. This is the physical genius. He's nothing short of a beast!

LEARNING MODALITIES

Audio—Coach, please talk to me. I need to understand it intellectually. After that, I will be able to translate it into my swing or delivery. I am smart and this is the way I learn best. I actually read instructional manuals before I use electronics. I am a nerd.

Demo—Its crazy how some people can be a 300 hundred pound hitting coach. I mean if you are unable to demonstrate, there are going to be a whole lot of players you cannot help. They need to see it done and that's just a fact. At some point they are going to need to see you actually get off the bucket and show them! Or find someone who can help with demonstrating. Utilizing video of good swings can be helpful. Showing bad swings can back fire in their psyche as it doesn't re-enforce or strengthen neural connections. *See mirror neurons.*

Media—Photo Sequences, Charts, Video, and Diagrams are very helpful for the visual learner. Most people learn this way.

LEARNING PROCESS

Fitts and Posner documented that learning a new skill happens in 3 phases. Cognitive, Associative, and Autonomous.

Cognitive ability is the mental process that the brain uses to perform a movement such as the mechanics of hitting, throwing, shooting a basketball, et cetera. With age, one's cognitive abilities begin to fade and the ability to carry out certain tasks goes with it. Hence, there are no 45 year-old shortstops in baseball (yet). And for younger people, if you're not careful, you could lose it if you don't use it. It is believed that mental exercise, such as puzzles, reading, learning languages, and playing musical instruments, are key to maintaining and improving cognitive ability in both children and adults.

Neurons are the conduit that transfers a signal at a very fast rate. In fact, it is the function of the nervous system.

MIRROR NEURONS

> *"Visual Content Marketing rules the internet . . . the brain is elastic. It learns, changes, and adapts."*

Yes. We have special circuitry in our brain that helps or hurts us whenever we look at each other. Some of my students that I spend a lot of time with will recall me saying,

"When you go back to your team, don't look at your
teammates swings—you might start swinging like them."

Why would I say that? Because when you look at someone else doing something, your neurons fire almost the same way as if you were doing it yourself. Hence, Americans love to watch sports. Men jump off the couch when a touchdown is scored. Women cry during movies. The fact is, we connect through vision or watching. Its almost like we are actually doing the act. So for mirror neurons, seeing and doing are the same—the brain/ mind cannot always distinguish between the two. Think about how babies and humans—first they *look* and then they *do*. And how many little boys do you see who have the exact same walk as their fathers. Or daughters who brush their hair or laugh exactly like their mom. For example, I like to demonstrate when I teach, and I see many of my hitters swing similar to how I would swing. Not in a cookie cutting way, but the similarities are obvious. So mirror neurons connect us to the world in which we see— connecting us to the movement and feelings of others. This is why hitting is contagious.

I'm trying not to make this a science book, but it's hard to ignore science when we are breaking down the deeper layers of performance. We have to understand the mind of the performer. So the brain is elastic. It learns, changes, and adapts.

In fact, in my hitting classes, I try to match up new students with veteran students so that newbies can learn from more experienced hitters.

See it—This phase involves seeing one's self actually doing the act. Visualizing or seeing yourself doing it can only happen after you really understand the parts. A good question to ask yourself is do you get it?

Do it—This second phase of the learning process is about connecting the parts into one complete action. This should not be rigid, but smooth. After plenty of reps an athlete will know what does and does not work, as trial and error is an important factor here.

Perfect it—Development of the new moves to the point that they become an instinct. Proper instincts are programmed into the psyche and body by proper training and reps—thus making it automatic. It takes some athletes more time and reps than others to get to this point.

These are the Cognitive, Associative, and Autonomous phases of learning.

Here is a great exercise to try: go down to your local schoolyard and watch a 3rd grade kick ball game. Within 15 minutes you will see a lot of things:

1. You will see who the better athletes are. They stand out. It is really like night and day. Those athletes you identify as elite will be the best athletes in every sport. These children are faster, stronger, more athletic and simply more aggressive than their peers. And they don't look over at their parents every 2 seconds. It's really interesting.

2. You will also see the players who struggle with basic skills and coordination. This can only be improved to an extent but usually at a slower pace. These athletes will need a ton of reps and training, just to maintain a level of mediocrity. Without hard work this athlete will go from mediocre to terrible, as they get older.

3. You will also see the sore losers, quitters, leaders, selfish, lazy, superstars, etc. This is where confident athletes begin to separate themselves from the fearful athletes. It begins in the schoolyard. Do you remember how you felt when they picked sides in the playground? Were you a first round draft pick or were you the last one picked? Were you the one picking teams? Were you organizing positions? It makes you wonder if leaders are born or made?

CHAPTER 2

Take It Personal: Seven Personality Types and their Manifestations

Before I get down to the main point of this chapter please understand that this is more of a *biology* chapter than a *psychology* chapter. So what does biology or psychology have to do with hitting? Well we know that psychology is the study of the mind, behavior, and the mental processes. We also know that hitting is something like 80 percent mental (at least at the highest levels). We know that biology is the study of a wide range of life, specifically chemical and physical mechanisms of life. Without going too far into this, the portion of biology that concerns us most is physiology or functions of living organisms and their parts, namely you, the athlete/ hitter, the brain, the body, and how it moves or works together efficiently. My point is how does the mind, thoughts, personality, and emotions affect/ effect how athletes perform? And this is more of a biology issue than a psychology issue.

The one thing I never forget when it comes to developing athletes is that it's never business, always personal. Why—because first and foremost, athletes are people. Somewhere under that uniform, under the muscles and beneath the talent, there lies a person. And as a coach, you can run from that person inside of every athlete but you can't hide. The personality of an athlete has a lot to do with how they respond to development, and basically how they perform on the field. You will find that a lot of elite athletes, CEO's, and highly successful people are very much alike in so many ways. These are your Winners in life and they share a lot of common personality traits. The coaches that win year in and year out usually have the best people skills. They know how to relate to the *person* inside of the athlete in order to bring out their best qualities.

Athletes are going to possess a multitude of attributes: seven major personality types to be exact. However, one of these personality types will dominate their persona more than the others but they will all be there.

The 7 Athletic Personality Types: the social, the intellectual, the physical, the emotional, competitor, the dejected, and the indolent.

Which of the 7 Athletic Personality Types dominate your persona? Every team has a combination of different personality types. So does every workplace, church, school, et cetera. Identifying those people and dealing with them on their level is the key to getting the most out of them. It is the key to success.

What part of an athlete am I developing/training? Can I profile the human side of my players in order to develop the entire person?

1. THE SOCIAL ONE
(NICK SWISHER, DENNIS RODMAN)

Loud, talkative, needs to be around people, loves the game but loves the social aspect of team sport just as much, craves attention, eccentric.

2. THE INTELLECTUAL ONE

Quiet, reserved, can be with the crowd, or alone, a thinker, can go and take batting practice without a partner.

3. THE PHYSICAL ONE
(BO JACKSON)

A very high level of (AI) athletic intelligence, translates new information from brain to body quickly and with greater ease, clearly surpasses all others in ability, doesn't really have to work as hard as everyone else, the natural.

4. THE EMOTIONAL ONE
(PAUL O'NEILL)

Believes he should get a hit every time up, doesn't handle failure well, may take the last AB in to the next one, wears her emotions on her sleeve, gets really high when she wins, and very low when he loses, cry baby.

5. THE COMPETITIVE ONE
(KOBE BRYANT, MICHAEL JORDAN, DEREK JETER)

Driven by their will to succeed, wants to be the best IN EVERYTHING, hates to lose, probably works too hard, may or may not be very talented. Cannot relate to and has a low tolerance for lazy losers. Selfish in a good way.

6. THE DEJECTED ONE

The defeated, insecure one. The one who lacks confidence. Loner and socially maladjusted. Underachieves in every aspect of their life.

7. THE INDOLENT ONE
(CARMELO ANTHONY, ROBINSON CANO)

Great control of their emotions, laid back, often mistaken for lazy, even tempered.

Please note that each manifestation is not always true about each personality type. For example, every emotional player is not a crybaby and every crybaby is not necessarily an emotional player. I am finding that an athlete can be any combination of these seven major personality types. And sometimes an athlete can evolve into or develop different personality types later on in their careers. Many times personal situations or new social environments can contribute to a change in personality types or which type dominates their personality and when.

For example, one can be social or the social-competitor. There are also in-box personalities.

IN BOX (OR IN-GAME) PERSONALITIES

HP1: Patient-Aggressive—the athlete that is poised and experienced enough to wait for the right opportunity and then be aggressive enough in their pursuit to make things happen.

- Knows his strengths
- Understands her weaknesses
- Waits for her pitch
- Aggressive when opportunity presents itself

HP2: Passive—the athlete that takes patience to a whole new level. This is the one who waits too long and then tries to be aggressive when it is no longer called for.

- Takes the first 2 pitches
- Over-Analytical
- Unsure of one's self
- Unable to pull the trigger
- Not a 4th quarter or late innings player
- Not very clutch

HP3: Over-Aggressive—the athlete that over does everything. They swing too hard. They chase change ups in the dirt on the first pitch. They always foul out of games. They take ill-advised shots from out of their range. A risk-reward type of athlete.

- Swings at too many bad pitches
- Bad decisions
- Swings too hard
- Steps up in the clutch
- Catalyst

HP4: Self-Destructive—when you meet this person's parents you will know why they are the way they are.

- Negative Self-talk
- Always finds what is wrong
- Focus on the bad
- Never acknowledges the good
- Eg., 0-4 with 3 line drives and gets depressed

HP5: BA—the badass. Every championship team needs like 3 of these. There is no way you win a championship without at least 3! Seriously. BA's are fearless and step up in big situations. They don't care who the opponent is. In their minds, they are always better than their opponent. BA's strike out and walk back to the dugout like they just hit a HR. *(see Play Like a Bitch/Boss Chapter)*

- Lives for the big moment
- "Bring it On" Mentality
- The one you want at the plate in the last inning
- Fearless
- Bullet Proof Confidence
- The perfect amount of cockiness and humility
- Hates to lose as opposed to loves to win
- You want to go to war with this person
- Plays Like a Bitch/Boss

HP6: QBA

The Quiet Badass

- Natasha Watley, Mariano Rivera, Angela Tincher
- Silent but deadly

THE DIVA COMPLEX

"So gifted, its become his greatest asset and his absolute number one liability."—Colin Cowherd on LeBron James (before the ring)

Let me begin by saying that athletes are not born with Diva Complexes but parents, coaches, media, etc, create them. Children become what their circumstances allow them to become. As adults, we have a choice about what we will allow. For example, if a young player strikes out and throws his bat in frustration, and as a coach you allow that, then it is your fault when they are unable to manage their emotions later in their careers. Too many coaches allow the best players on the team, to get away with things that are simply unacceptable. You are an enabler and hurting that player by fueling the fire of their immaturity. They will not be able to cope with adversity later on.

So the Diva has always been the best player on the team or the best player on the team is always the Diva. Which one is it? Didn't really have to work too hard, but still dominated. In contrast there is the grinder, the one who worked twice as hard and never realized the same success. So Michael Jordan could get cut from his high school team and develop the spirit of a grinder and Lebron James could be worshipped at 16 years old and develop that fighting spirit later in his career. Now it becomes more evident why the Pac-12 conference has 400 championships. West coast athletes are raised with the spirit of a grinder. Are East Coast athletes the most spoiled? As a parent, do I love my child less if I am tough on them? As a coach, if I kiss my best player's ass, am I really helping them? For more information on the Diva Complex, see the New York version of Alex Rodriguez or Dwight Howard.

CHAPTER 3

Natural Emotions: Controlling the Feeling

Later, we will look at Neurons and Cache and how these two factors influence how we respond in performance. In fact, within the brain to body process, there is a point where visual stimuli are filtered through our emotions. An example of visual stimuli would be the pitcher's arm and the moving ball. So our in-box personality, how we feel or what we believe about specific stimuli, are crucial to how we respond to it and our approach to collision. Reasoning and emotions go together, as does gut instincts and intuition. In fact, the same part of the brain that controls emotions, also controls memory. So there is a direct correlation between what you are feeling emotionally, to what you remember about something *(in this case a stimulus)*. This in turn, affects how you perform in a particular situation.

Emotions such as sadness, anger, pleasure, fear, and worry are normal but these do have extremes:

NORMAL-EXTREME

sad—depressed
angry—unprovoked aggression
pleasure—addicted
fear—anxiety, phobia, panic, choke
worry—generalized anxiety disorder, freaked out, melt down

EMOTIONS—Our thoughts, feelings, likes, dislikes, comfort zones, etc., Pertaining to the thought-life of an athlete. Particularly the thoughts that determine how we see ourselves or our circumstances and positively or negatively affect our performance. Emotions are shaped by our experiences, how we remember them and how we choose to respond to them. Emotions will manage you if you do not manage them. Make a choice. Ask yourself,

"How am I going to deal with what I am feeling today?"

Emotional Intelligence, Emotional Balance, Emotional Resilience, Emotional Command, and Emotional Momentum have the ability to change the meaning and the intensity of the visual stimuli. Our emotions shape our perceptions of the stimulus. Take a look at the following definitions:

EMOTIONAL INTELLIGENCE

According to EQI.org Emotional intelligence is the innate potential to feel, use, communicate, recognize, remember, describe, identify, learn from, manage, understand and explain emotions.

EMOTIONAL BALANCE

The Balance of our Emotions as it relates to focus and performance. Most people get too happy when they are doing well and too depressed when they are struggling. The experienced and mature athletes realize they are not necessarily their results and the struggles are only temporary.

EMOTIONAL RESILIENCE

The ability to rebel against the relentless knock of your emotions. Emotional Resilience is your ability to cope with stress and change, without having a melt down. Emotional resilience, to a degree, is something you are born with. You can go to a playground and pick out the children who have it or don't. Even toddlers who pout and cry every-time they don't get their way.

EMOTIONAL COMMAND

The ability to demand your emotions to be subject to you and you not become subject to your emotions. Can you take a punch? You are pitching and you just served up back-to-back home runs. I know you feel like crying but your teammates don't need to see you crying right now, so you command that emotional reaction.

EMOTIONAL MOMENTUM

What is Emotional Momentum? It is the reason why teams play well or play terrible. Especially young teams or women's sports. So scoring first is key. Lead off walks, hit batters and errors in the late innings is a definite emotional momentum shift often times leading to a big inning, walk-off defeat, or come from behind victory. Emotions are what great coaches are able to manage in their players. Protecting your team's momentum is the key to winning and it begins with their emotions.

THE MELT DOWN

Many teams are like ice cream. Actually, most pitchers are like ice cream. The moment a little bit of heat is applied to the situation, they melt. Think about what happens to ice cream when it melts. First you have this heap of frozen sweet milk. Then all of a sudden with a little bit of heat or pressure the meltdown begins. It loses its shape. It loses its form. It's not the same as it was before the heat. Heat changes the entire situation. I often sit at the game and wait for the melt down to begin. Most pitchers will meltdown when the situation gets too hot. Rarely, do you see a pitcher bring it up to another level in the face of adversity. There are only a few, and many if not all of them have won championships.

Hitters melt down too. In fact, hitting is all about the rally. Many people say good hitting is contagious, but bad hitting is also contagious. I believe that great coaches are really good at creating an atmosphere for great hitting. The psychology of the 3rd base coach is so important. Here, I am listing the different types of 3rd base coaches that can kill the spirit or Emotional Momentum of a would be hitting team:

THE PSYCHOLOGY OF A 3RD BASE COACH

1. The Hitting Coach
This is the 3rd base coach who needs everyone to know how much he knows about hitting. He tries to give the batter a hitting lesson in the batter's

box as though this will actually help. He fails to realize that the game is for the players. And if he says something valid and the hitter actually gets a hit, he feels the need to take credit for it. *"See I told you. See what happens when you listen to me."*

2. The Comedian
This is the 3rd base coach who constantly makes jokes and sarcastic remarks that are embarrassing to the hitter. These remarks never help the hitter. It only aggravates. Honestly, it makes the hitter not even want to look down 3rd base for a sign. If half of these coaches have ever played the game, they would never do this.

3. The Humiliator
This is the 3rd base coach who can never be positive. He is always finding something wrong with what a hitter does. Instead of giving a hitter the much-needed confidence in the box, he is always ripping the batter or making the batter feel inadequate. This is a confidence crusher and part of the reason good hitters may struggle with confidence. Eg., Everyone knows the hitter just swung at a pitch over their head. Why announce it at the top of your lungs? The hitter is trying to turn the page, but you (the coach) won't let it go. The Humiliator feels the need to pick at every single thing. This is never positive. Ever! If you don't believe me, then humble yourself and ask your hitters.

4. The A-hole
Basically, if you are a 3rd base coach and you need so much attention during the game, you probably have all three of the attributes above. If you possess all three of the attributes above, then you are a certified asshole. And believe it or not, this is why your hitters are performing below their potential. Learn how to shut up if you can't be positive. Speak to them after the game or between innings about small adjustments they should make. The game is not always the time for it, especially while they're in the batter's box. In fact, if you watch the top 10 college teams or even MLB 3rd base coaches, they NEVER give hitters so much as a negative body posture. They realize the importance of confidence and focus for the hitter's maximum performance. If you want to rip into your hitters, do it in private and stop showing them up. If you think they aren't trying or aren't good enough bench 'em or cut 'em.

5. The Eunuch
This is the 3rd Base coach who basically gives everyone take signs with 2-0 and 3-1 counts. This coach has no confidence in his players and manages

in fear of failure rather than instilling confidence in his players. This coach will also sac bunt with the number 3 or 4 batter early in the game.

6. The Cowboy

This is the 3rd Base Coach who has about 3 pages of signs and kills rallies by putting on ridiculous base-running plays such as the 'fake-bunt-hit and run-delayed steal,' with the number 3 batter in the first inning with a seven run lead after you have batted around.

Reminder to players: Some of you are realizing success in spite of your 3rd base coach, not because of them. Too many of you are using this as an excuse for your failures. Stop being so sensitive. You are probably going to have coaches further along in your careers that are worse and you still have to perform. This game is what you make it. Do not allow anyone to define how much fun this game can be.

CHAPTER 4

IMAGINATION: A Lost Art

"Real isn't how you were made," said the Skin Horse, "It's a thing that happens to you."—Margery Williams, The Velveteen Rabbit

Seems like the younger we are the more we believe we *can*, and the older we get the more people tell us we *can't*. I'm wondering how do we get people to stay younger in their minds so that they really believe they can do more? So it would appear that the older we get, the further away from invincibility we go. The older I have gotten, the more I realize I can never fly. Think back to when you were younger and you felt as though you could actually fly. You were invincible. Remember those days? The only limitations you had were those placed on you by *concerned* adults with their fears. Why is it that adults want to protect kids from failure and wonder why they can't succeed when they get into real situations and can't cope with or bounce back from failure in competition?

Competitive anxiety is born here—right in this situation! It seems like we are conditioning athletes to be mediocre. You can't even make an 8 year-old do pushups without getting arrested. And when the 8 year-old turns 14, we wonder why (after all the training he has received) he doesn't have the guts to swing the bat in a clutch situation.

"Get down from there." ....
"You're gonna get hurt." ....
"Don't swing, you might miss." ....
"Swing softly so you can put it in play." ....
"Don't swing at change-ups until 2 strikes." ....

Seems like someone was always telling me what I couldn't do. Good intentions obviously, but it stifles optimism.

Just the other day I was watching two younger players pretending. They were pretending that one was the batter and the other was pretending he was a pitcher. One child was pitching from a full wind up and throwing an imaginary ball to his friend who was in his batting stance with an imaginary bat. They began to argue because the child who was pitching said he struck him out and the batter said he hit a home run. He was actually running around the bases and the pitcher was trying to tackle him to keep him from ruining his strikeout. Of course they were boys. And I am sure that game was just as real for them as it would be if they were in a real game. So I'm wondering how as we get older, we lose the ability to daydream and imagine and be able to pretend. The skill of imagining is so much apart of life success. I am learning that there is a fine line between reality and the surreal world some people can create for themselves.

I often tell my students that the best hitters have great imaginations. For the purposes of teaching hitters how to implement the skill of *imagining* into their hitting, I have defined *imagination* as pre-playing your future. I am also defining *memory* as replaying your past. Hitters actually replay pitches they have already seen and pre-play pitches that are in-flight. Then they match the two with the present pitch, in order to anticipate where contact will take place.

When I was about 16, I remember how hungry for success I was. I used to go downstairs into the basement of our apartment building in New Rochelle. I stole a traffic cone from somewhere and that was my batting tee. I hung an old blanket from the pipes on the ceiling and hit balled up socks. The socks were quiet so I would not wake my neighbors. I can remember how every swing I took felt like it was a real hit in a real game with real results. Now that's imagination. And when I got up in the actual game, I felt like I had done it a million times already—and I had.

Memory and having a good one, is photographic. It ties directly into recognition and being able to predict movement on a pitch and eventually the area of contact. So let's say a pitcher who throws hard, blows one by you—if you have any sort of memory, you record the speed of the pitch and adjust your timing. This will help you to not repeat history. Or if a pitcher throws you a better than average rise ball, you can also adjust your swing to meet the ball or even lay off if it's out of the strike zone. Hitters that repeatedly swing late and never adjust to velocity or movement are simply not skilled in the memory of movement. See *m.o.c.* in the perfect collision.

Now imagination is the pre-play. We are now seeing what the ball is going to do before it does it. We can determine a clear and accurate sense of the spot where the speed and trajectory of the break-angle is taking the ball—and meet it there. The more pitches we see (remember/memorize), the better we can imagine or predict contact area.

CHAPTER 5

MIND vs. BODY

*"There are more players that have the talent to be the best
in the world than there are winners," "One way of looking
at it is that winners get in their own way less. They interfere
with the raw expression of talent less. And to do that, first
they must win the war against fear, against doubt, against
insecurity—which are no minor victories."—Tim Gallwey*

I think we all can agree that so much more of the grind is mental for athletes and the skill of combining our physical and mental skills is the biggest challenge for us all. In fact, most athletes never understand how to get to that place—that place where the physical plane and the mental plane become one. Unmanaged emotions get in the way most of the time. Some athletes can get to that place some of the time and very few athletes get there most of the time. Helping athletes to understand this reality is something I pride myself in teaching. I make certain that every aspect of the presentation (drills included), involves a mental and physical challenge.

So this morning, I asked myself the question, *"Does the mind follow the body? Or does the Body follow the mind?"* Now keep in mind that this is a debate that philosophers have been having since before Plato and Socrates. But I could only answer this question based on my own experience and I wanted to relate it to sports performance and realize that it is also relevant to life performance. It seems that the answer to this question is counterintuitive. The Mind definitely follows the body but in some instances the body must follow the Mind. This happens to be different in different players, and in different situations. For example, here are college softball players who have:

- Played at top 20 division 1 softball programs
- All-Americans at least twice in their college careers
- Players of the Year honors in their respective conferences

P1, Melissa Roth, Louisville
P2, Allissa Haber, Stanford
P3, Amber Flores, Oklahoma

In working with these 3 players, my approach had to be so different with each one due to the fact that they all process instruction totally different.

P1 actually had her own ideas or strong convictions about hitting and I needed to give her a certain amount of space to "do her own thing." This is what worked for her. Roth has a strong personality and needs to feel the process out for herself. I kept my door cracked for her and would only drop subtle advice to her in passing in the dugout or I would sense when she needed me as she would come stand next to me after an AB.

P2 is totally different form P1. She is an extra BP type of hitter. You have to kick her out of the cage during pre-game. However, Haber is more of an intellectual and really benefitted from our talks in the cage more than the actual swings. She has a need to want to talk things out and visualize the process in her mind first. Then she is able to bring it to the game swing.

P3, a combination of different personality attributes, was hard for me to figure out on any given day. Amber has so much confidence, and an unorthodox approach that our talks were almost never about hitting. We talked mostly about boys, relationships, and life issues. Sometimes I would ask her if she had *checked out* on me or was she still with us. I recall throwing her a 5-hour energy and saying let's go. Or she would come back from an AB and I would say, *"WTF was that? How the hell were you player of the year in college?"* And she would agree and rip a line drive her next AB.

During the summer of 2010 I had the privilege of coaching these players as rookies in the NPF, a women's professional fastpitch league. Neither of them played like rookies and they all adjusted well to the pitching which was very different from what they had dominated months before in college. There were other rookies, during that season that I thoroughly enjoyed. However the three I mentioned clearly outperformed the others. Not because of talent, but attitude towards development. They were very coachable in their own way. Somehow I was unable to crack the code with the other rookies, although I was willing. It hurt to watch them fail, especially when they would not allow me to help. I could say that a teacher is only as good as the student, but in retrospect, I should have done more for them.

CHAPTER 6

FOCUS: The Ultimate Operating System

Are you confusing routine with focus and commitment? So many athletes have this checklist of what they DO but its meaningless if their focus or operating system isn't updated. Assuming one has talent, the following chapter applies:

> I feel like focus deserves to have its own chapter. There are so many definitions of focus and what it is or should be. I wanted to take the time to perhaps give you a different perspective.

Got Talent? Got Skills? Got Genetics? But when it comes to personal choices—you Got None!

For some of the most talented individuals you can sense that they fail just based on their operating system. I will give you an example: you can take the latest and most sophisticated computer hardware and software, complete with the fastest processor, 4GB of memory, et cetera. Turn that computer on and you will have a blank screen without the proper operating system running. In the mobile phone world, the three most popular OS in the mobile phone world are Google's Android, Apple's IOS, and Blackberry's RIM. In the desktop world it would be Windows on your PC or OSX on your MAC. So then what is an athlete's operating system?

An athlete's operating system is their attitude, work ethic, commitment and mainly their focus. Focus seems to have so many different interpretations so let's talk about *true focus* here. I know many people feel as though when the game starts, there's nobody more focused than they are. And that may be true, but true focus is about what you do off the field. And I am not talking about how many swings you take or how many times you go to the gym per week. I'm not even talking about how many times you go to your hitting coach. Those things are important, but without an appropriate operating system, you are like a BA Sony computer with a blank screen—not so BA after all.

Q: So whom do you hang out with? They say we are a reflection of the top 5 people we spend the most time with. Evaluate those five people. How many of them are really losers? Seriously. If you're not like them, why hang out with them? And if it is a struggle or a sacrifice to avoid them . . . if it is really hard to not find yourself with these losers, then you are not focused. You probably won't ever be truly focused. I hate to say it, but it is likely that you are a loser just like those five.

Q: How disciplined is your training regiment? Or are you just a member at a gym and showing up wasting time bouncing from machine to machine? Do you actually challenge yourself? Do you have goals for improving strength and speed? Are those goals specific to your sport and realistic for your body type? Really? What are you doing?

Q: What do you eat? I see so many athletes sign their letter of intent and then become overweight. That is not focus. That is just crazy. After the signing is the time to work even smarter.

By the way, if you struggle with the above questions then you simply aren't focused. Or your level of focus can be better. Your level of focus should match the level of play you are preparing for. So if my goal is to play baseball at Arizona State and I am on the high school basketball team and the volleyball team, attending every social event and running for class president and two other committees . . . need I say more? If you're not focused, you're distracted.

Now focus is merely one of seven virtues every BALLER needs to have. The other 6 support Focus. Thus there are:

SEVEN VIRTUES OF A BALLER

THE HIDDEN VIRTUE OF FAITH is so necessary because without it one would only pursue that which they can see. The thing about Faith is that we never see what is to come, whether failure or success. But with Faith, we stretch our minds to imagine things most could not, in order to achieve higher degrees of existence. So our thought process is king here. The virtue of an athlete is true character shining through. Character is not to be confused with morals and values. *See below.*

1. CHARACTER
Knowing the difference between morality and character. So one can take extra batting practice, extra grounders, eat right, go to bed early, and give to charity, and say, "Hey look at me, I am the perfect player." This same person will turn around and wish their teammates failure, talk back to their parents, and talk crap about their coaches. Proving that morals are for everyone to see, but character is hidden and a matter of the heart.

2. HUMILITY
Whether forced or by choice it is the realization that it's not about you, but the team.

3. DISCIPLINE
This is self-discipline or self control. Discipline by itself is as simple as getting up every morning and going to a workout or refraining from certain people, places, behaviors, foods, et cetera.

4. CONFIDENCE
Unconditional. Not depending on past failures. See Bulletproof Confidence.

5. RESILIENCE
No matter what, we get tougher. We bounce back no matter what! No matter what!

6. FOCUS—aka The "F" word
True Focus begins off the field.

7. PATIENT-AGGRESSIVE
Learning to attack the opportunity that you waited for when it presents itself. This is a personality trait that probably cannot be taught. It is something that is learned through your experiences and circumstances growing up as a child. If a hitter is too patient they will take too many pitches and miss opportunities. If a hitter is too aggressive, they will try to force opportunities that aren't there and fail.

I always think of patience as a weapon—a weapon of virtue. I was sitting on my couch one day watching this special on National Geographic called, "The Amazon's Deadly Dozen." One of the predators was the Bushmaster

Snake, which happens to be the world's largest venomous snake. The narrator made a comment about one of the Bushmaster's virtues in saying that its patience is its deadliest weapon. I thought that was simply profound.

And my desire is that my hitters, like the Bushmaster, will learn how to wait for the pitch they are looking for, anticipating, or expecting, and then crush it! The Bushmaster is also known for its aggressive attack. John Rittman, former Team USA and current Stanford Softball Coach frequently uses the term patient-aggressive. He wants his hitters to be patient and aggressive at the same time. Not an easy task when the emotion of the game overcomes you but it is an excellent mental approach.

CHAPTER 7

The Perfect Collision

"The great ones begin at the end, and then work backwards. Now they know the path to the desired result because in their minds, they have already been there. And on their way back (there), it is easier to stay on course because the road is so familiar."—Rob Crews

Think about the way a GPS works. The GPS needs the final destination before it can actually chart your course. I am finding that great hitters have the ability to see their perfected swing with the perfect timing and create that perfect collision in their *mind's eye* first. The great ones don't start at the beginning and find their way to an end result—that's how we get lost. Instead, they actually begin at the end result or begin at success—and from that starting point they can find their way back to the finish line—the desired result, success, or that Perfect Collision.

Therefore, good hitting will never be a swing, but always a mindset. We see the swing on the physical plane but there are layers that lie beneath the swing that occur in which we can never see. The perfect collision begins first with the ability to access and duplicate your perfected yet *personal* thought process. An athlete's personal thought process originates in the mind and then surfaces to where we can see and feel it. I believe in the possibility of the *perfect collision*. I believe that when everything happens perfectly—that is, on time, with the right angle, and great extension, hitters can experience a sort of NIRVANA or the *perfect collision*. Hitters and hitting coaches will forever attempt to define The Perfect Collision. Here, I am going to attempt to bring some sort of order to the process by which many "hitting guys" spend countless years attempting to perfect. So much of it is physical but most of it is mental. And for female athletes it is more emotional—yet there is another portion that is visual. In fact, hitting always begins with the eyes. Hence, there are 4 phases of the swing. Let's call these the Fantastic Four.

If the sequence below is true, then recognition is king among focus topics in training for hitting and most sports where reaction is the major factor in performance. The Fantastic Four happen in this sequence:

1. EYES RECOGNIZE

Eyes track, read, and lead the rest of the body. True timing really happens here. Not everyone has the same visual abilities. For this reason, two people with identical swing mechanics and similar athletic coordination will not hit with the same consistency. A hitter's hand speed and barrel accuracy/efficiency are a direct result of great eyes or Visual Speed. Coordinating the eyes with the hands and barrel become more difficult at higher levels of play—mainly because there is less time to evaluate and predict point of contact. Visual Acuity is the one variable often overlooked, and under-developed at every level of competition.

2. HIPS ENGAGE

2 and 3 can happen simultaneously. The Kinetic Chain or flow of energy from the ground up through the back foot (big-toe) up to the hip flexor is a reflex that power hitters must learn to harness correctly. Positioning the back foot to move in a specific direction results in how efficient the hip flexor can transfer that power into the barrel.

I think so many good hitting coaches get stuck on what a swing should look like and limit how many hitters they can make better. The realization that hitters will vary in how they look and still get it done is important for being an effective teacher. You learn from hitters who may do things differently (and still get it done), and then you can help more hitters to be successful and help you actually win games. Its funny how so many people wanna be a "hitting guy?" A real hitting guy is never stuck on one type of swing. A real hitting guy understands that there are a whole lot of ways to "get it done." I mean, that's the whole point anyway, right? Getting it done? Or would you rather a hitter continue to do it "your way" and never grow?

Back to my point of the hip or the engagement phase. You will be reading about that next, when I further explain each phase. But I need you to be as open-minded as possible in order to understand it.

1. BRAIN DECIDES

The brain evaluates pitches (in-flight), anticipates angles, and decides the best possible angle to contact. The brain is able to make these calculated predictions of the point of collision based on visual stimuli and years at bats and stored data—I call it *cache*. See IFF's or In-Flight Factors. We will discuss IFF's later on in the book.

1. HANDS COMMIT

The Hands react/respond to whatever the eyes perceive. Now the word perceive is tricky because there are so many different perceptions. Three different hitters can have 3 different perceptions of the same pitch. The correlation between the eyes and hands is what makes a hitter good. Period!

Eyes **RECOGNIZE**	Body **ENGAGE**
Brain **DECIDE**	Hands **COMMIT**

FANTASTIC FOUR: DIGGING DEEPER

Recognize
The first phase or what simply has to happen first is the Recognition Phase. Here's the funny thing about Recognition (please remember): It is impossible to recognize something you have not already seen *(hence the prefix "re" meaning again)*. And it is easier to recognize something you see a lot. Let me explain why that is so profound and of the utmost importance. For all those who jumped on the "numbers on tennis balls" bandwagon, we do not track numbers on tennis balls in a baseball or softball game. In fact, tennis players don't even do that. People can get pretty good at recognizing numbers on tennis balls if they do it enough. But hitters need

to recognize red seams and ball spin—not numbers. With numbers on tennis balls, there is no recognition happening—at least recognition that is relevant to hitting a baseball or softball. Later in the book, when we get into cache, we will further establish this premise. For now, let's agree that recognition only occurs when we see something we have already seen before. But whether you agree or not, Merriam-Webster agrees with this definition of recognition. So if I see a person in the mall who looks familiar to me I may say, *"I recognize that face from somewhere."* I cannot say that I recognize him if I have never seen him before or at least someone who resembles him. Hence the prefix "re" again.

The word recognition comes from the root word recognize. According to Myetymology.com, the Latin word *cognoscere (to know; become acquainted with, aware of; recognize) re means back or again.* Therefore we cannot recognize something we have not yet seen. We can only recognize something that we have seen before. If I see someone on a plane that I recognize, then I have most likely seen him or her before or someone who looks just like him or her. And since we are not hitting tennis balls with numbers on them in the game nor are we playing in a virtual game on a screen, what is the point of all this B.S. out there? Ask a neuropsychologist or a neuroscientist. I did. In fact, I asked 6 of them—and they all agreed.

Now great hitting coaches realize that we can evaluate a gifted hitter by her hand-speed. Great hitters have great hands, or fast hands (whatever your terminology). But hand-speed is birthed out of visual speed. See it (or recognize it) sooner: react (or respond) sooner. The faster the eyes: the faster the hands.

So then what is visual speed? So many people have fast hands but would never know it because their eyes are way to slow. Some people understand the dynamics of the eye muscles. Soft or quiet eyes make for better tracking and HD recognition skills. Like any other muscle, when eye muscles are less fatigued they perform better—they perform faster. Some people get this while others must be taught this. So what are we teaching? Players with great swings but poor visual skills will struggle—even with the perfect swing. The eyes lead the body, period!

This is the reason why bat-speed is overrated. Because you can have a fast bat and not comprehend timing but have a slow bat and actually understand timing. And the slower bat hitter can be the better hitter, the same way most fast runners are terrible base runners and get horrible reads and jumps. The key is having the ability to *read*, which makes your bat speed relevant. There's that word *"read"* again. High-level athletes are actually *speed-reading*.

Let me give you an idea of how fast the brain and mind are. There are some neurons that can fire about once every 5 milliseconds, or about 200 times per second. Over 100 billion neurons are communicating with each other during the process of performance. Recognition happens during the read. So as a hitter reads a pitch, she also recognizes and cross-references the pitch with every spin-pattern, break-angle, and break-speed, she has ever seen or is stored in her memory/cache. This is why hitters who come from mediocre levels of competition can't hit at top 25 college programs. They don't have enough cache or pitches stored in their memory. They have not seen enough elite pitching to compete at the elite level. Some hitters see the ball while other read the ball. Which one do you think great hitters do? See or read?

Once upon a time I used hand-speed as a gauge to evaluate and measure the upside of a hitter. The hitters with the best hands are/were the hitters with the best hitting potential or ability. Quite naturally, fast hands are a result of great visual skills. The hitters with the faster hands are anticipating and evaluating pitch type, velocity, movement, and location so much sooner. It's visual. And this visual information processing is possible because high-speed neurons fire and communicate this visual information, which in turn creates more accurate responses in performance.

I remember how visual I was in grade school during the learning process. I would receive my vocabulary list and memorize the order of the letters and when I saw the word again, I knew it. Did I really know it or did I merely memorize it and recognize it? I rarely sounded out a word and actually read it—at least not after the first encounter with that word. I merely memorized words or parts of words and because my recognition skills were above average, I became a great reader. I did the same thing with basic math—especially multiplication tables. So hitters who actually attempt to read a pitch in this sense (as they would sound out a word) will always be slower in their response. Yes always. But hitters who have memorized the movement of a pitch will be superior in their reaction time. I am saying that bad hitters are actually sounding out pitches and good hitters already know the pitch. In fact, as a hitter, when you see a pitcher for the first time you should be *sounding out* his delivery and pitch trajectory from the bullpen so that when game time comes you can actually read it!

An example of this is hitters who *take* change ups early in the count or early in the game for that matter. These hitters are never going to be able hit that same change up later in the count or later in the game. Why? Because those hitters have not had the experience of the miss, in order to eventually perfect the timing and recognition necessary for the perfect collision.

Engage

The second phase of a swing is the Engagement Phase and where anticipation happens. The engagement is much like pre-marriage. It is safe to say we are on our way to, or moving toward commitment because we are in *yes mode*. But we can always say no or decide not to commit. The engagement phase is the pre-commitment part of the hitting approach. In this phase, a hitter isn't totally committed, but moving towards or anticipating commitment. Without getting into mechanics, this is the phase of the swing where hitters drift (big toe to middle toe) or begin to move towards positioning themselves to be fast enough (in their back hip flexor) to hit but giving themselves the option to take the pitch if they need to. This part or phase can precede the *read* or happen at the same time. More advanced hitters will evaluate a pitch and come to a conclusion about what that ball is about to do during this phase (see IFF's).

So many hitters who "squash the bug" or spin, are committing the hips and hands at the same time, not allowing the evaluation phase of the process to happen correctly. These "spinners" make their bat shorter on the outside pitch, pull outside pitches to middle infielders, miss low pitches, hit a lot of long foul balls, and separate improperly. I usually like to say the hips (sometimes the hands) will engage. However, it is the hands that commit. Commitment is the fourth phase, which we will see later on.

Decide

The third phase of the swing is the Decision Phase. Because the evaluation part of the swing has already happened (I hope). Here is where your brain has to make a decision as to where contact happens. I like to say that the prediction or the anticipation of the actual moment of contact is visualized or intuited. Great hitters will actually see contact before it happens. If you are a great hitter, then you know what I am talking about. Don't believe me? Ask a great hitter. Anticipation is the reason why we can't be hyper-focused on the ball but we should be focused more out in front of the ball.

Reading numbers on tennis balls, while encouraging focus and attention, re-enforces lateness in anticipation. If you are still visually focused on the actual ball past the halfway mark, you will not be able to catch up visually for efficient anticipation and prediction of contact. In essence, you are sounding out the pitch and not speed-reading.

Deciding (a mental process) and reacting (a physical process) do not happen at the same time but its pretty darn close. In fact, deciding happens during the approach or slow movement of the hands toward the point of collision. If you are committed, then you swing faster, if not then you can stop the swing. Therefore, the decision making phase is really an anticipation phase and a function of the brain—purely instinctive. Basically, a hitter only needs to be able to make one decision—and that is NOT to swing. Since a hitter is already in "Yes-Mode" and has already decided to swing before the pitch is even thrown, "No" is the only decision to be made in this phase. This anticipation along with the decision happens during the *read*. Decisions are made based on the accumulation of visual information (good ab's) or the accumulation of visual mis-information (bad ab's).

In the Decision Phase there are four In-Flight Factors (IFF) that every hitter must consider. IFF's are learned not taught. Advanced hitters have already completed the IFF checklist at phase 2. Keep hitting and playing and you will get better in these areas. There are so many IFF's, possibilities, or variables.

IFF-1 What is it?
IFF-2 Where is it (going)?
IFF-3 How to get there?

What is it?
IFF no. 1 or the ability to determine pitch-type and pitch-speed. Two necessary factors for predicting contact and arrival time. Determining pitch type and probability of the break is definitely learned—not taught. The more curveballs you see, the better you will become at hitting them. Reading specific pitches and recognizing them early comes with experience. So again, reading pitches is learned and not taught. This is anticipation of arrival time and destination or AOC, which I called Anticipation of Collision.

Where is it?
IFF no. 2a or the ability to identify the ball earlier in its flight. Also the ability to get on the front side of the ball visually. I usually want my hitters to have

the ability to establish a visual route (VR), which will bring them back to the throw-zone before ball release. The throw-zone is the area where pitchers release the ball. I purposely didn't call it a *release point* because that varies according to the pitch and or pitcher.

Where is it going?

IFF no. 2b is the difference between seeing and reading. Hitters who see the ball only know where it is. Hitters who read the ball can better determine where it's going. Hitters are able to jump or move from one point to another with eye movements called saccades. *Anticipatory Saccades* are ideal. Moving from the area of ball release to the front part of the ball allows a hitter to anticipate much sooner and with greater precision.

How to get there?

IFF no. 3 is really more about anticipation than it is reacting or reaction. Having the foresight to determine or predict precisely how the collision is going to happen is the key here. Here, the hitter coordinates the proper hand path and bat angle based on the visual information.

Commit

The fourth and final phase of the actual swing is the Commitment Phase— the act or non-act of the *Decision* that you made in phase 3.

We know that the hands commit. Hands instinctively create the proper bat angle necessary for the best possible contact. This instinct of creating the angle (AOC) is learned over time with experience and reps. Evaluation of hitters based on hand-speed is really visual speed. Everyone has fast hands but fast eyes makes for even faster hands. Fast eyes help hitters to make decisions sooner and more efficiently. The instincts of the hands to the ball are a result of visual speed and visual accuracy that can actually be developed in all hitters through the tempo and sequence of the swing movements. These instincts are also developed and maintained by certain drills. See Anticipation of Time to Collision (ATC) and The Seventeen (front elbow and bottom hand).

CHAPTER 8

Cache and NeuroMechanics

*"If you are distressed by anything external (or internal),
the pain is not due to the thing itself, but to your
estimation of it; and this you have the power to revoke
at any moment."—Marcus Aurelius, 167 A.C.E.*

Cache is just my fancy word for files. Let me begin this chapter by stating that primary cache is learned and then re-learned—stored and then stored again. With every new level an athlete attains comes new files, memories, or cache. Secondary cache is not learned but rather taught. Now it is not my intention to turn this into a science book although everything we do in sports performance is based on nothing more than science. It is necessary for me to explain certain scientific phenomena related to brain to body communication otherwise known as or what I would like to call the *NeuroMechanics of Hitting*. In reality, one could say the NeuroMechanics of Performance because the organization of thoughts and movement are applicable to just about all types of human performance.

Athletes, especially hitters that are *neuromechanically* sound, should play the game as though they have the answers to the test. Everyone else is competing blindfolded. This brain to body communication happens because of neurons which transmit data faster because of cache or information in the form of stored visual data from past experience. A normal human brain has over 100 billion neurons. Neurons respond to visual stimuli. Within the hitting process this stimuli would be entirely visual. Most hitting coaches deal only with the swing itself and not the dynamics that determine how and why we arrive at a particular swing. The way in which we react, respond, or swing is determined by visual stimuli and our interpretation of it. So the neurons communicate the presence of visual stimuli to the central nervous system via electric impulses. This data is then processed or cross-referenced with stored data and sends responses to the hips and hands for the appropriate action or response—the swing. There is a unique set of neurons created for every pitch, from every angle, against every possible background, at every speed, from every trajectory, and every distance you have ever seen. This is cache and crucial to our ability to anticipate and achieve greater sweet spot accuracy. And for this reason tee-work and front toss from short distances can translate to in-game timing and success much better than machine work. I have not used a pitching machine in my entire career as a hitting coach. Never will.

Here is another example of how cache works: I was having some difficulty accessing certain web pages on my website and called my Webmaster. He instructed me to clear or empty cache and try again. When I did that, it worked. I thought it would be interesting if I could bring this word, "cache" from the computer world into the world of sports, performance and motor learning. A good definition of *cache* is a block of memory that is temporarily stored for future access and faster retrieval. So whenever you visit a website, your computer's web browser stores that webpage's information so you can get back to that same page faster. Without stored cache, future visits to that same website would take longer. In sports and player development, we need to get the brain to store our experiences so when we repeat those experiences, our brain can access it and the body can coordinate the correct response—faster. This is a function of brain to body training and memory recall. The Talent Code, by Daniel Coyle, one of my favorite reads, the author shares how certain talent factories are developing phenoms with master teaching and deep practice techniques. Deep practice or targeted struggling to accelerate the learning process.

Here, I am simply defining cache as memory. But it is memory that is to be accessed quickly. A hitter has two types of memory, which both work together—primary cache and secondary cache. Primary cache is temporary memory such as a pitcher's pitch types. Hitters store this data as primary cache for quicker access for a particular game or upcoming series. For example, a hitter may take pre-game batting practice against a left-handed pitcher in order to prepare for a lefty who is throwing in that particular game. Secondary cache is more permanent and is where a hitter stores his hitting mechanics and various approaches. Also, secondary cache is where templates for movement patterns, sequences, and in-flight adjustments are stored for more natural instinctive access—vital for efficiency in anticipation. The neurons associated with primary cache open communication with secondary cache. Secondary cache stores pre-determined responses sort of like templates which chart courses for hand path and barrel angles for that perfect collision—bat to ball. Therefore batting practice becomes two-fold; we are perfecting parts of our primary cache and re-enforcing secondary cache.

Another example of primary cache is a hitter's ability to visually-mentally record a pitcher's delivery and synchronize the replay with his own timing system. And because every pitcher's delivery is different and every hitter's timing system is unique, the two must be synchronized. The better hitters have a gift or special talent for timing or synchronization of their own timing system with the delivery of each pitcher they face. We are now perfecting better ways to help hitters understand and execute this process faster.

You ever drive to work or school or some familiar destination—a place you've driven to 1000 times before? Sometimes you get there and you don't even remember driving past about 2 or 3 exits or streets. That is secondary cache. I have had hitters tell me after a home run, that they don't know what pitch that was or where that pitch was. Now that's what I call automatic—a result of great primary cache.

VISUAL CACHE

Imagine 3 hitters:

> Hitter A has seen 200 curveballs in batting practice yesterday.
> Hitter B has seen 200 curveballs in batting practice 6 months ago.
> Hitter C has never seen a good curveball.

Now imagine all 3 of these hitters playing in a game against a really good curveball pitcher. Hitter A has more recent cache stored in his memory. Hitter A hits the ball hard and has good AB's.

Hitter B has less recent cache stored but after his first at bat, Hitter B will be back to where he needs to be. Hitter B can retrieve that stored cache and get back to where he needs to be.

Hitter C struggles. But the positive side is that Hitter C is developing and accumulating cache for future access and success. In fact, Hitters A and B also went through their struggles before gaining the confidence they needed which really came from their individual failures—which is now cache. Failure is important, because we learn what does not work and translate that information into future opportunities.

It is for this reason that hitters who have the opportunity to play in warm weather for 12 months a year, will have a deeper database pitches and pitchers. Hence, more opportunities to fail and learn from that failure. You can't teach experience.

PHYSICAL CACHE

Cache is the reason why Michael Jordan couldn't hit in professional baseball. He didn't have enough of it. There are players in professional baseball who have stored cache from the age of 6. They have taken hundreds of thousands of swings. Cache is also the reason why certain college coaches only recruit from certain travel teams that play in certain tournaments, and against certain levels of competition. In certain skill sports, there are particular brain-to-body cache that must be formed at a certain age or it becomes very difficult to establish it later in life. For example, there aren't many chess masters who have begun playing competitive chess after the age of 8 or 9. Nor are there many exceptional hitters who have not played competitively before the age of 11 or 12.

Visual Information Processing Chart

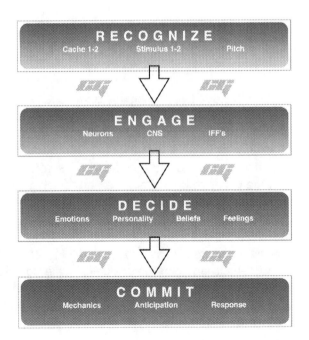

CHAPTER 9

Creating the Perfect Collision
(9 parts)

*"The visual process involved in the recognition phase is
really about what information your physical eyes are able to
match with what you are replaying in your mind's eye. The
hitters who do this well can hit better than everyone else."*

As we saw back in the Sikology chapter, there's a bit of a challenge for
today's athlete to bring new concepts or movements from the brain to
practice and especially from practice to the game. Seven years ago, before
the brain eroding distractions of texting and social media weakened their
focus, it was easier to get hitters to absorb concepts, apply them, and
make adjustments within 5 minutes or at least 5 sessions. Now it seems
like it takes a player 5 months to master the simplest of tasks. I am learning
that this blockage or delay of learning and implementation is mostly due to
brain-body disconnection. And who holds the smoking gun? Not only social
media, text messaging, video games and all the other distractions today's
youth have to content with, but bad-teaching techniques. Consequently,
I have been researching and creating test studies with young athletes
around the country to develop a training model for baseball and softball
hitters that accelerate the learning process. I call it *OptoGaze™* and the
focus is connecting the brain to the body in the areas of balance, control,
and coordination while enhancing efficiency in timing, angles, and proper
extension necessary to maximize potential for power hitting.

One of the problems many hitters and coaches face is the amount of time
it can take in the developmental process of a skill. With every level, there
comes more of a challenge for hitters to master sequence, tempo, and
direction of swing movements. Therefore, we have developed the most
comprehensive, accelerated training system for developing athletes by

re-connecting the brain to the body where there is often a disconnect or delay in the process of creating that Perfect Collision.

In this segment I will outline the various ways in which a hitter goes about creating the perfect collision. So much of it is visual and or involves the use of one's imagination. I am finding that visual skills or the ability to visualize are the primary factors for barrel efficiency and accuracy. **The visual process involved in the recognition phase is really about what information your physical eyes are able to match with what the memory or the mind's eye can replay.** The hitters who do this well can hit better than everyone else.

Understanding angles and swing planes are a direct function of a hitter's ability to anticipate contact areas within inches or even centimeters—and doing so at certain speeds. This is a skill that requires a hitter to have an acute *"sweet spot awareness."* There is a series of mental and visual tasks that occur in this process that happen in a specific sequence that I have outlined into 9 major parts. Organized thoughts and the ability to compartmentalize specific mental and visual tasks are what allow for consistency and ultimately greatness. I wouldn't call it multi-tasking but more like the ability to focus on one thing. Unfortunately, modern social dynamics have re-shaped how we now define focus. In a world where texting at a restaurant or cinema is the norm, how do we get young brains to become more focused? Since the trajectory of learning has changed, the trajectory of teaching must change as well. In order for us to be effective in teaching to the new more evolved brain, we need to be more creative in our approach.

Below are the nine parts of a Perfect Collision grouped into 3 trimesters. At the end of these 9 parts, the perfect collision is born. Before we can even go into ROC, we begin with ROC, but the hitter has already seen a pitch or seen this pitcher before. One cannot recollect something they have never seen or experienced before.

ROC

The *Recollection of Collision* is a hitter's ability to recall, remember, or replay the speed, trajectory and break angle of a pitch (therefore, they must have seen it before). We are calling that stored memory or cache. *Recollection comes from the Latin recollectus to gather again.* The more times a hitter has seen a particular pitch, the easier it is to recollect or remember it. We have already discussed how primary and secondary cache and ROC are intertwined. This is a fact and proves that a majority of hitting at a higher level is learned and not necessarily taught. For this reason, the warm-up is important in all sports. The bullpen session and the pre-game practice are vital to the player's success. The pre-game recalls and gives the player access to what they may have lost to short-term memory in terms of speeding up the eyes, hands, and other body parts. For this reason I disagree with pre-game tee drills. I believe the ball should be moving unless you are working on something specific. Most hitters who have not hit live pitching in a while need a few AB's to remember or re-program their triggers, timings, visual cues and sequences. It's sort of like a reboot or refresh. Players, especially hitters from warmer climates have seen more live pitching and played more games, hence they have more cache. Or shall I say they have *better cache.*

As part of her pre-game routine, Jessica Mendoza will often stand-in against her own pitchers' bullpen sessions in order to visually prepare for the game. Also, hitters who have 6 or 7 pitch AB's have seen more pitches and will have better timing on the 8th pitch. That's why I can never understand why pitchers throw the same pitch twice in a row and in the same spot. Stupid. Especially to a hitter you know is good. That might work in the bottom of the batting order, but certainly not in the middle.

VOC

The *Visualization of Collision* is an ability certain hitters have where they can see the path of a pitch before it actually happens. In other words, as the pitch is coming in, the hitters with great VOC have actually pre-played the path of the pitch and see it as a delayed moving image. I know that sounds creepy, but it happens. In this scenario, the actual ball is really a replay of what the hitter has just pre-played fractions of a second ago. The skill of being able to zoom in and out at the right time is crucial for a hitter to master this.

AOC

The *Anticipation of Collision* happens when hitters can eliminate certain possibilities of a pitch (while in flight) in order to guesstimate the proximity of contact. In other words, if a hitter is able to learn the break speed/angle of a pitch, the hitter can determine destination of pitch and proximity of collision. Anticipation is important for quick decision and response—it is the act of mentally leaning or drifting towards a pitch without actual commitment.

In fact, it is because of AOC that teams recruit different types of pitchers and strategically change pitchers in order to give hitters different looks or trajectories throughout a series of games. For example, a team may recruit pitchers who do not throw hard in order to follow harder throwing pitchers, which can frustrate hitters by keeping them off balance.

POC

The *Prediction of Collision* goes with anticipation or AOC and is the confirmation of a hitter's commitment. This prediction is based on visual information that was already gathered from VOC and AOC. Accurate predictions come from accurate visual information—leading to great body timing. On the other hand, bad predictions come from visual misinformation and lead to bad swings.

ATC

The *Angle to Collision* is really hands-lead-barrel or the barrel remaining behind hands. VOP, AOC, and POC are crucial to a hitter's ATC. If this is accurate, then the hitter will be closer to a 45-degree angle between the forearm (of the top-hand) and the bat just before contact. Players who are closer to a 90-degree angle are positioning themselves to go around the ball. 90-degree players are usually casting out or straightening their front arm to soon (see angles and prepositional training). Many times, the difference between a ground ball out and a double in the gap is about the length of .5 balls (in softball) or .75 balls (in baseball).

TTC

Time to Collision has to be the instinct that comes from Athletic Intelligence or just plain old coordination. IYCA defines Athletic Intelligence (AI) as *"the capacity for learning and understanding various physical skills and how they relate."* Some people are not as Athletically Intelligent as others. They will learn things slower or simply never get it. In order to ascertain TTC, one must possess AI. So many hitters struggle with the understanding of how to put it all together to create proper contact or a perfect collision. They never progress to the *Do It or Associative* phase of learning. So the *Perfect It or Autonomous* phase will never happen. As coaches, we know when things will never happen with a player no matter how hard they work. ATC is usually where most hitters get lost or where their potential is revealed. Their angles and concept of how contact should happen is never realized visually or mentally (see VOC and AOC). Putting all of the correct body movements, tempos, and sequences together in one swing and creating the ideal angular approach gets us closer to the perfect collision.

TTC involves knowing the exact time of the moment of impact (at least within .5 softballs or .75 baseballs length and understanding how to make that moment happen. In order for efficient TTC to occur, a hitter needs to calculate when and where the collision will happen—**and then get there**. Remember that ATC or the angle to contact is vital to the outcome or exit speed, trajectory and spin of the ball from the bat.

ETC

Before we can even talk about ETC, let's define extension first. Extension is everything (good or bad) that happens after contact.

Extension thru Collision is the ability to stay behind the ball after contact or stay through it. So many hitters believe that the swing ends at contact, when in fact it is only the beginning. Hitters who can feel ETC will keep their barrel behind the ball longer. I often refer to this as allowing the barrel to chase the ball after contact. *Extension and Power* should be synonyms when we are talking about hitting.

Most hitters who do not realize proper ETC are simply swinging a short bat due to the front shoulder headed into the dugout behind them too early. The longer a hitter can keep the shoulder in, then the longer the length of their bat can actually be, especially on the outside pitch and the low pitch. I often refer to hitters with short bats as hitting with their bodies and not their hands. Also, hitters that allow the top hand to roll prematurely are changing the direction of the barrel. Hence, extension cannot occur naturally.

DTC

Direction thru Collision or what I sometimes call Directional Extension. I see so many swings where players have what appears to be extension but with a trained eye, you will see that they are so far away. The key here is a hitter's ability to stay behind the ball no matter what direction the ball is going. So if the ball is going to right-field, then so should the barrel (post contact). If the ball is going to left-field, then so should the barrel (post contact). Players with top-hand release should stay on the bat with two hands until both arms have extended or straightened out. Top-hand release should not normally occur before the bat passes your front foot. There are of course exceptions.

MOC

Memorization of Collision is necessary for hitting a pitch the next time you see it. Usually, a hitter will increase their chances of creating the perfect collision when they have seen a pitch more than once. The more times you see it, they better you should be at timing it. MOC is the key for this to occur. MOC brings us back to beginning of our circle ROC. Variables or attributes of different pitches are read, categorized, and stored for future access and faster recognition. It then becomes cache. This is the real reason baseball player's cannot hit softball pitchers. They just simply have not seen enough pitches from the hip and cannot visually adjust fast enough. For them, it is a strange and unfamiliar cache.

CHAPTER 10

FIVE DEMONS of a Bad Collision

"Missing a pitch doesn't always mean you swung through the ball. In fact, the worst miss is the miss when you actually hit it—you just hit it wrong."—Rob Crews

I guess my first question to you is do you believe in demons? In religion, the occult, and folklore, a demon is a supernatural spirit or being that inhabits an individual and influences them to do evil or bad things. Or is it man's way of placing the blame for their own issues on something apart from themselves? Well, whatever you believe, it's still a demon either way.

The definition of a hitting demon is based on the notion that the perfect collision is good and perfect. And whatever causes the eyes, brain, body, hands, or barrel not to create the perfect collision would have to be a hitting demon. I am going to identify the five demons of a bad collision, their causes, manifestations, and how to exorcise them.

When I think of demons, I think of how I can exorcise or get rid of them. There are many hitters, especially younger hitters who feel as though contact and making contact is the name of the game. They feel like if they are able to put the bat on the ball, then they have achieved a degree of success. The mentality is, "Well at least I didn't strike out, or at least I didn't miss." The truth is an out is an out. In fact, a lot of hitters feel like they have failed if they swing and miss. Strike one is always better than oh for one. And the last time I checked, we get 3 strikes. You don't always have to use up the 2 free strikes, but sometimes you may need to. In short, we are looking for the best contact or angles to create the perfect collision. Just putting the bat on the ball isn't always good enough.

DEMON	MANIFESTATION	CAUSES	EXORCISE
D1— Barrel under ball (BUB)	• Pop up • Foul back • Miss	Straight front-arm early in the swing, Hand-path of down to forward, Barrel below the hands during in-flight approach	Higher Hands in setup, Back elbow in the hip slot. Hand Path straight to the ball
D2— Barrel over ball (BOB)	• Ground Ball • Chop • Miss	Too much down in the swing, never gets level, Too linear too soon	High Tee Drills
D3— Barrel around ball (BAB)	• Ground Ball to pull side • Foul Ball to pull side	Top hand rolls over, barrel leads the hand, front arm casts or straightens to soon	Tee Drills w/ Tee closer to the body while hitting the ball up the middle
D4— Barrel late to ball (BLB)	• Foul back • Chopper type ground balls	Front foot lands late, big stride, casting out, looping, exaggerated bat wrap	Take away or shorten the stride
D5— Barrel early to ball (BEB)	• Foul ball straight back • Ground ball to SS • Foul ball pull side dugout	Visual misinterpretation of TTC, anxiety	Mentally adjust the objective opposite field

So basically, what I have done here is come up with 5 imperfect collision symptoms. Each symptom has its root in the visual process of the swing. It is visual flaws that cause these 5 demons to exist.

Exorcises not exercises are actually drills that can help remove or exorcise mechanical flaws in a swing. Because so many hitting flaws have their root in the visual process, we can't see them; we only see their manifestation. They are invisible.

CHAPTER 11

21ˢᵗ Century Definition of Hitting

*"Hitting is Timing, Consistency is Angles,
and Extension is Power."*

If someone were to ask me what the definition of hitting is, I would have to begin to answer that question with what hitting is not. So let us first establish what hitting is not, in order to make way for a clear understanding of what hitting really is. Hitting is NOT the perfect swing, for there are many people who have great swings and still can't hit. And I can flip that by saying that there are many people who can hit, but have not so perfect swings. So if I teach someone how to swing properly, I did not necessarily teach him or her how to hit—only how to swing. Now I know what you just read, probably challenges what most people think or have thought or read in books or instructional videos. But I have come to realize that after one has acquired the perfect swing (if this even exists), they have accomplished about thirty percent of the hitting process. Let's talk about the other seventy percent.

So the definition of hitting is three-fold. Hitting is about being (1) On-Time, (2) with the Proper Angle or Swing Plane, (3) and Extension or the correct post-contact Direction. Therefore Hitting is Timing, Consistency is Angles, and Extension is Power. I have found that there are two ways in which we can help hitters to be ON-TIME. We develop timing by improving (a) Visual Skills, (b) Front-Foot discipline. There are also three components of developing and maintaining Power in the Swing: (a) Bat Lag, (b) Hip Flexor Speed against a Strong front side, and (c) Extension. And finally our Emotional/Mental Game determines how consistent we can be.

The first thing I do as a hitting instructor is assess what the immediate issues are. I always establish short-term goals for myself first, then the student. There are always issues that I know will take months, and then there are also issues that I know will take minutes. The willingness of the student to learn and their individual passion level always determines how much I can help them. By myself, I am nothing to a student. But the student must bring passion. And with passion, comes work ethic, and with work ethic focus, and the other necessities for overall success—especially in-game success. The bottom line is that the student has to care more than I do. The student has to care more than their Dad does. This is passion. How do we gage passion? We can gage passion by level of commitment only—especially off-field focus. There is no other way to tell.

TIMING

So lets take a look at *Timing*. Hitting is Timing or one's ability to be on time. People who have been around me for a significant amount of time know that this premise is the primary basis for the Complete Game teaching model. I structure all of my focus with students around this as primary because even with the perfect swing and the strongest body, without timing it is impossible to be consistent. Timing is even more important than bat speed. What's worse than a fast bat that's late? Perhaps a slow bat that's on time. We need both speed and timing.

The two elements of timing I am most concerned about are *recognition,* and *front-foot discipline.*

Great hitters understand that they are timing two things in a sequence: the pitcher's body, and then the ball. We are defining this as *Stimulus 1* and *Stimulus 2*. As a hitter, I need to be accurate in syncing my body tempo with the pitcher's body tempo, and then my hands with the ball. Thus is the reason why separation is important. Too many hitters are combining the stride with the swing and never realize separation. Without good separation, accurate and efficient timing cannot be realized.

RECOGNITION

Recognition is the first part of timing. With improved recognition skills, comes the ability to be on time. I like to say that there are 2 types of hitters visually—those who *read* the pitch and those who *see* it. Hitters who *read* the pitch can anticipate where the ball is going and hitters who *see* it react to where it went. Certainly, we cannot objectively measure visual speed and how quickly a hitter can get to the front side of a moving ball. However, an experienced coach will be able to discern hitters with great eyes.

FRONT FOOT DISCIPLINE

When stride lengths are more controlled and timely, then timing is easy. So many hitters don't realize the importance of establishing the front foot as firm, planted, or anchored early in the process. Actually, this should happen before commitment but generally happens at the same time—this is the problem. Now this is an oxymoron for sure, because while the swing should remain connected, there must be a *separation* of stride and actual commitment (of the hands). So what is often referred to as *"toe-touch"* is and should be followed by heel plant. Heel Plant should be completed before the snapping of the hip flexor in order to maximize front-side-stability for power. Toe touch is the landing of the front foot for hitters that actually have a stride. *(See chapter 14)*

ANGLES AND PREPOSITIONAL TRAINING

I have found that I can gauge an athlete's ability to be successful based upon they're understanding of angles to the ball. Believe it or not, some hitters just cannot intuit that. I have seen college hitters who don't get it, but 10 year-olds who do. That's weird. Some hitters are genius with respect to vision and hand paths and others seem as though they don't understand it. Prepositional Training helps hitters to develop a better feel for the angles necessary to maximize power. I believe this is learned and not taught. But once you feel as though a hitter is getting it, you can re-enforce it.

Drill:

In *prepositional training*, I spend the majority of the training on giving the hitter the task of hitting the inside part of the ball no matter where I pitch it. The players who can intuit this are at a particular skill level—a higher skill level. The barrel control or barrel precision is the focus. If you are training a hitter who is struggling with barrel control in 5mph front toss, then as a teacher you have a real challenge. This hitter will struggle with taking the instruction from the brain to practice or tee work. So taking it from practice to the game is a long shot. However, I have seen players who have worked for 4 years and then in 1 week begin to "get it" literally overnight.

Hitting the ball in certain spots goes along with this as well. So many hitters are mis-interpreting where contact should take place on the inside or outside pitch. This can either be a visual problem or simply talent deficiency. And if I can be real here for a second, these are the hitters we usually say suck. The ability to match the proper angles in hitting is an instinct and developed through repetition in what I like to call *Focused BP*. Some might also call it "deep practice." During Focused BP we are beginning the session with a purpose and sticking to that purpose throughout the session. There is no room for jumping around to other issues. It is just plain old focus—which seems to be a lost art.

POWER AND EXTENSION

The Complete Game Hitting Model stresses the significance of extension and how it is the origin of true power. So many hitters believe that contact is the end of the swing but power hitters understand that contact is just the beginning. In fact, the greater the extension, the greater the power. I'm finding that it is easier to achieve extension with top-hand release but not impossible with two hands on the bat throughout the swing. It is a matter of what is comfortable and works best for the individual hitter. I have never made one or the other mandatory. Obviously with younger hitters, safety and the possibility of a flying bat is an issue to consider.

How can a hitter who is not physically strong, generate more power? The answer is yes. Power is more about mechanics, which helps us to execute the power that we already have. Body position, especially the leg position, determines hand path and influences proper extension. I believe that the number one hitting issue in Fastpitch Softball is that players are not swinging hard enough. It is the fear of missing that causes hitters to make contact the priority.

CONSISTENCY

The Mental Plane is all about managing one's emotions. Once a hitter gets to the point where they are just no longer concerned with pleasing everyone. No longer concerned with failing or afraid to fail. Once a player gets this CHIP on their shoulder so to speak, then they are ready for the next level. Until then, players will always play with a certain reservation.

You get to a point where you just don't give a hoot anymore. And you're like, *"LETS GO! BRING IT!"* (But is it more than just cliché?)

I often make reference to the idgf mode. My hitters that are reading this know exactly what I'm talking about. Idgf is an actual level, in idgf mode there is no fear—only confidence and aggressiveness. In idgf mode, you are a playmaker and not subject to the circumstance but the author of the circumstance. If I just lost you, then you are not there.

I can see it in my players. I know when they have changed. I know when they have figured out that part of the game. This is where guts and heart come into play. Form and mechanics won't save you. The pounds you have lifted in the weight room have nothing to do with this. Your brand new 24-karat gold composite bat means nothing. This is about removing all fear and canceling all doubt. This transformation is the source of bulletproof confidence. For some, it is a permanent gear and others will shift in and out of gear.

My question to you is do you have another gear? And as a coach, can you activate another gear in your athletes? Some players play better when the consequences for failure are greater. Its not that they weren't trying before that, they just know how to access and activate the ability to go into a higher gear. This is why most people love to watch playoffs and Olympics. It is truly a display of high-level athletes playing under the highest amount of pressure—in short, there is so much more at stake. It is a battle of the best versus the best. Not a whole lot of mediocrity in the post season. The significance of the playoffs is that it's the best teams and the highest stage—a real test of what an athlete is made of. So what is your batting average on Sundays or elimination day? Let's talk about that. Not how many home runs you hit against Team DADDY-BALL GOLD.

In the book Complete Game, I made reference to the ability to flip the switch—an internal switch into a higher level of intensity. When you're playing against a rival or one of the best teams in the league, its different. I would rather watch the Yankees play the Red Sox or Texas play Texas A&M. I know the players will either really show up or wet the bed.

As for me, I always ran faster when dogs were chasing me. And I think pitchers especially will pitch better against a good team or in a tight spot than they would in less significant situations. I don't believe being competitive is as black and white as most people think. There are levels or layers of competitiveness. Perhaps Competitive 1 and Competitive 2—almost like gears. Not that I am trying harder or lesser but I am bringing my a-game in certain situations. Like who would want to face Manny in the late innings of a close game? He is just a different hitter in the clutch. Are you?

FLIP THE SWITCH: PLAY LIKE A BALLER-BOSS-BETCH

A.Y.I.B. (Accessing your inner-baller-boss-bitch switch)

"For people who don't watch anything on TV more offensive than the Disney Channel, the word bitch is used here as a general term and not to bring down the value of a woman. A true woman's value can never be brought down—especially not by a word."

Be honest, doesn't the word BETCH sound a hundred times cooler than bitch? Playing like a Betch is something important to the elite female athlete. Just as playing like a Baller or Boss is important to the male athlete. Yet most people hate their boss or have bosses that are bitches or very difficult to deal with. And most bosses, at least the successful ones, are not really very nice—so we categorize them as bitches. Hence, the phrase, *"My Boss is a Betch!"* No—your boss is being a bitch because she has to be in order to get it done. You need to learn how to be one too and maybe you can get something done for once. At the company Christmas party your boss is probably a nice person. It is an on-field character trait that is mastered by few. The person is playing *like* a bitch, but it doesn't mean she *IS* one. To be *LIKE* something, simply means there are similarities but when you take a closer look, there are distinct differences. The player just knows how to get into character. You are playing *AS* a Bitch would play.
For some people it is a whole lot easier to transform into a bitch. For others, it is too extreme of a personality change. They are simply too nice to be a competitor. You ever coach those players that are just so nice and play the game well and therefore don't really *COMPETE*? So are you competing (boss-bitch) or are you participating (nice guy)? Nice guys bat eighth.

Question: How confident are you really?

Example: Go look in the mirror and say this to yourself, *"Hi, my name is Jody Johnson and I'm a BA."* And if you're a male *"I'm a freaking STUDD."* Then ask yourself, *"Am I convinced?"* I am not talking about pointless positive self-talk. I am talking about really believing it—really knowing you're a BA and then going out and proving it.

The bottom line is you need at least two or three BA's or Boss-Bitches on a team to win a championship. The good girl or nice guy act just won't get you there. You will probably do well in life—maybe or maybe not. The lack of badassness is precisely why you continually do not get it done— especially in the big spots. So if you skip this chapter please know that you are missing your password to success at the next level. If you don't believe me, ask any big time player or championship team. What do you think big-time competitors are thinking in their minds when they are killing your team? Trust me, they are not thinking friendly thoughts!

I'm finding that certain *athletes* no matter the sport. Scratch that. I'm finding that certain *people* no matter the profession, activity, or task, have an innate ability to access a certain level of focus at will. There is an inner *baller-boss-bitch switch* that they're able to flip. And some can access yet another switch beyond the first switch. This is why the *Boss-Bitch* is not an employee. He is in charge. Are you in charge? Are you in control? And if you're not in control, then who is?

Some people just aren't competitive or cocky enough to be a Boss-Bitch and their passive personality takes over during the moment. Thus often results in passivity and ultimately failure. So I'm learning to identify this personality trait and (if they work with me) literally exorcise it from their in-game mindset. A lot of it is upbringing and environment. We can't help where we are from or what our circumstances are and unfortunately one cannot go out and buy a mindset. You either have it or you don't. It is innate. But can you fake it? Absolutely! But only to an extent.

Players have become and are becoming less competitive daily. Too many games—too many tournaments. 0-4 no big deal. We play again next weekend. My team is a showcase team so I don't have to really earn playing time, so why work hard. My coach owes me at least 3 innings a game. If I get benched for being mediocre my psycho-mom will send my coach a 10-page email. Yeah this is the reality of the situation. What do you honestly think is better, 50 showcases and no skills or 25 showcases, more training, and better skills? I never thought I would see this day. What have we done or should I ask what are we doing? It's embarrassing.

The Gladwell Theory backs up the previous paragraph. I believe that most people are already familiar with Malcolm Gladwell and the 10,000 hours rule. If not, let me bring you up to speed. Gladwell maintains that in order to achieve success in any given field, one must have put in at least 10,000 hours of practice.

I will say this. What makes the baseball or softball player who lives and plays in warmer states a better? Well for one, they can play in more games against better players in a given year. In the colder parts of the country, only the psycho/aggressive people can gain that type of experience. Of course those who have the resources (like cash) and can afford the proper training and travel to warmer places to play more games. Hence more high-level basketball players come from colder parts of the country and are not distracted by warm weather activities and beaches.

So this 10,000 hour rule—how much of it is games and how much of it is practice? Games are an example of primary cache and practice is an example of building secondary cache. Practice without the right feedback is just as irrelevant as games against mediocre competition. You can practice all you want but without the proper feedback you are just not going to improve as much as you can with a knowledgeable coach or teacher. And you can play all the games you want to but if you are competing at level B that will not prepare you for the next level the same way that competing at level A can. You can't apply to Harvard without taking certain steps and courses. If you disagree, then take your child out of AP courses or private school—and after that go and move to the hood. Yeah, I thought so. I wonder why people compromise quality in sports but not in other life activities. Dads who know nothing about hitting will attempt to teach their kids to hit but then hire a tutor for math and piano. What is that? Well the bottom line is environment influences and contributes to growth and success. Are there exceptions? Absolutely, but there are also rules. So you see we have all these variables. And to take it a step further, there are obvious differences between D1 and D3 athletes and starters and non-starters—athletic ability, genetics, and talent being the obvious. There are also levels of focus and commitment. How many practice hours and how many games have been played against good competition? How many games against mediocre competition? So how stupid do you think college recruiters and pro scouts are? Well, I happen to know how intelligent college coaches and scouts are because I have friends that are in the business. And there is a reason why some of them will never come to certain tournaments or recruit from certain teams. If you shop on Fifth Avenue then that's where you shop. And that's just how some of them, at least the winning organizations think. They are shopping or recruiting from certain levels—levels that are parallel to their college level.

While we are on the topic of training let's talk about strength and conditioning and it's importance. For the record, let me say that strength training is very necessary. When an athlete gets to middle school they should be working on getting stronger even if only pushups, crunches, and other calisthenics. The bottom line is in the 21st century, if you do not have a strength regiment, then you really aren't that serious.

There is also a flip side to all this. Some people are over-doing it. You have athletes playing in games sore and tired. If you want to win, that's just stupid. I mean your players aren't hitting more homers because you're killing them in the weight room, so what's the point? Has weight training become something to keep them busy so you don't have to deal with them? Look at your stats, you're slugging percentage sucks and you only steal bases with that one fast player who can't even get on base because he's too freaking tired from the weight room. We need to condition to the extent that we are ensuring that our athlete's bodies won't break down in the second half of a game or season. Ask yourself why you need your car to go from 0-80 mph in 2 seconds if the speed limit is 55? Just because Big School Tech is doing it doesn't mean it is right for West Tiny School A&M. I may not even have the same type of players. And what does the football trainer know about getting baseball and softball players ready for their season when he probably hasn't even seen a game? So how much is overdoing it? Can one over-train? Of course someone can over-train but the importance of recovery is what's most often neglected. Athletes need the proper recovery strategy that is appropriate to their body and their sport—pre-season, in-season and off-season.

The bottom line is if you're not playing like a bitch, then you're probably mediocre at best.

CHAPTER 12

Hitters and Connectivity:
The 17

What began as something for me to better understand some of the deeper layers of the swing has turned into a way for hitters to study their own swings and begin to ask themselves questions about their own approaches and comfort zones. Now this is something I do quite often with teams and small groups in order to get players to get *into* their swings. There are so many ways hitters can become disconnected in their swings. Without getting into them all, let's take a look at the most common 17. I refer to this as "the 17." The 17 most important ways hitters stay connected.

PROJECT OVERVIEW:

I email 'the 17' to the players. I can either have them work individually or in small groups. It can even be a competition.

I then explain to the recipients the following: *There are 17 major ways in which a hitter must stay connected. So many hitters become disconnected which can lead to mechanical malfunction. I want you to read all of 'the 17' very carefully and give each part the proper amount of thought. Then begin to think about the movements. You have to do this without standing or without a bat in your hands. You have to visualize 'the 17' first. We will discuss this in two weeks. By then you should be able to explain 'the 17.'*

By the way, the only way one can pass this test is if you get them all correct. If you get one wrong, you fail. You cannot consult anyone but yourself on this. It has to be all you.

3 exercises for coaches. Learn how to identify and articulate 'the 17.' Learn how to demonstrate 'the 17.' Come up with at least one drill to reconnect

each disconnection. Have the students submit a video presentation of their findings and then grade them on the project. This is an excellent way to promote initiative, bonding, and at the same time your hitters are learning about their own swings.

THE 17 WAYS HITTERS STAY CONNECTED

Action	Connection	Action
Mind	Body	Mind
Eyes	Hands	
Front Foot	Hips	
Bottom Hand	Top Hand	
Front Shoulder	Front Elbow	Bottom Hand
Back Elbow	Top Hand	
Back Foot	Front Hip	
Back Elbow	Front Elbow	
Top (Hand)	Front Foot	
Hands	Barrel	
Front Elbow	Bottom Hand	
Front Heel	Back Heel	
Back Foot	Back Hip	
Front Toe	Front Heel	
Front Shoulder	Back Eye	
Bottom Hand	Back Hip	
Top Hand	Front Hip	

THE ONE SEPARATION

We just talked about how hitters are connected in the swing. We really never want to be disconnected or separated at all. However, there is one time hitters must be separated in the swing and that is the separation of the stride/load from the hip snap. When these 2 are connected the results can be:

Loss of Balance—*It is impossible to maintain maximum balance without two feet firmly planted*

Loss of Control—*It is easier to distribute and direct power when you have total body control*

Loss Of Stability—*A stable front-side maximizes drive from the back-side and minimizes head wobble (and eye movement)*

Impaired Visual Acuity—*Efficient Visual Acuity relies on all of the above. Without those three, you're hitting drunk*

Loss of Power—*Balance, Control, and Stability contribute to maximum power. Without these 3, weights, shakes, and steroids won't matter much*

Late to Contact—*Many hitters have separation, but it happens to late*

Vulnerable to Off Speed—*Due to the lack of Balance, Control, Stability, and Visual Acuity, many hitters cannot stay back long enough to drive the off speed pitch.*

When we separate the stride (step or load) from the swing, we are separating our recognition system from our timing system. The two cannot happen simultaneously due to our human inability to multi-task those two brain functions. Hitters who put the stride (load, step or trigger) and the swing too close together are neglecting one. They are either on time with poor recognition or recognizing it with poor timing. In order to be consistent, we need both—and in most cases, they must occur separately.

CHAPTER 13

HITTING for Know it Alls

*You have heard of hitting for dummies,
well this is hitting for know it alls.*

DISCIPLINE OF THE FRONT SIDE

One of the most common recurring physical hitting issues is the lack of discipline of the front side. This issue is prevalent at every level of the game of baseball and softball. Players are either flying the front shoulder open or just plain spinning their entire body. Let's explore the front side:

Front-Side: Part-by-Part:

Lead Eye—the lead eye or outside eye should be level. Sometimes hitters hit upside down and cause the eyes to be uneven. We need level eyes during the tracking/reading process in order for the perception of the pitch to be accurate.

Front Shoulder—during the setup we need the front shoulder to be square to the pitcher and not the middle-infielders. The most a hitter would want to turn that shoulder in during the load or backstretch is about a few degrees. Hitters like Robinson Cano or an Amber Flores can get away turning in (more than a few degrees) due to superior visual and timing skills, but most (normal) people need to regulate this front-shoulder rotation.

Front Elbow—the front elbow actually leads the bottom hand as we read previously in "The 17." The front elbow leads the bottom hand, which assists in both hands leading the barrel. This is necessary for great bat lag and ultimately bat whip. On the contrary, when hitters allow the hands to lead the elbow you get the casting of the hands/arms and this births long swings.

Front Leg—the firmness of the front leg is crucial to power because the backside needs something to hit against. We don't want hitters to establish a strong front-side too soon, but flexion early on in the approach is good. The angle of the front-side or front leg should be tilted slightly in order for hitters to create the bat angles necessary for specific trajectories of ball off bat—especially backspin and lift-force—which are necessary for home-run power. Front leg tilt is also important for avoiding lunging or jumping at change ups and off-speed pitches.

Front Hip—the most common issue pertaining to the front hip is that many hitters tend to want to open too much or too soon. I like to see a hitter keep the front hip closed for as long as possible before it ultimately opens up. When the front hip opens, the front shoulder follows, then the front elbow follows, then the bottom hand follows, and then of course the barrel of the bat. The pre-mature opening of the front hip, shortens the bat hindering low-ball contact and opposite field power—however, keeping it (the front shoulder) closed longer maximizes at bat length, which makes opposite field power easier.

Front Foot—stride angles, stride distances, and stride directions vary. I am not sure there is one answer for every hitter.

Some hitters have more athletic ability and can time collision with more accuracy than others. Understanding when the stride foot should land (if it strides at all) is crucial to consistency. Timing of the landing of the front foot is most important for timing collision, stability and power. Hitters who understand that early front-foot anchoring will present more options and create more time to evaluate the pitch. Hitters who struggle with when this front foot lands will be limited as to how many options they have in their approach to the ball.

THE BACKSIDE, ROTATION, AND VCR'S

Much like videocassette recorders, extreme backside rotation is a thing of the past. There are still a few people who are rotating just as there a still people who are watching VHS tapes. If extreme backside rotation works for you, you should continue to do it. I am not against any style of hitting that actually works for you. I am pro-success. There are so many ways to be successful. I'm not saying that rotation does not or should not happen. I guess a good way to put it is that backside rotation, similar to breathing, is not something we should consciously think about but it should happen naturally. Check out how the sequence occurs in the outline below:

Back Foot (big toe)—
Back Knee—
Back Hip Flexor—
Back Elbow—

Hitters who have a tendency to rotate too much or too soon neglect this basic kinetic sequence, that is so necessary for consistent power.

RANDOM DEMONS THAT HINDER POTENTIAL

There are millions of demons that hinder potential—here are 31:

YOUTH PRE-HS LEVEL

Big Stride
No Load/No Negative Movement
Wrist Rollers
No Rotation/Too Much Rotation
Collapsed Front-Side/Weak Front Side
Hits Upside Down/Visual
Tension in Upper body setup
Mechanical or Robotic/Stop and Go
Late/Early

HS LEVEL

Late Start
Plays Basketball/Volleyball
Time Management
Weak
Tension
No Strength Trainer
Bat Selection
Too Heavy/Too Light

Ping vs. Composite
Too short/Too long
Full Head and Empty Bat
Hits 2/3 Balls
Front-Side Flies/Spins
Barrel Leads Hands/Casts out
Weak-Front Side
Too Mechanical
Mental Midget
Commitment Issues/Mentally & Physically

COLLEGE LEVEL

Visual
Form/Aggressive
Confidence
Happy Feet
No-Work Ethic
Mal-adjusted Socially
Partying/Lack of sleep
Inconsistent/No work ethic
Radical Changes by College Coaches
Mis-Management of Time
Pitch Selection

CHAPTER 14

FRONT FOOT: The New Trigger

"If you're not focused, you're distracted."—Rob Crews

The genesis or starting point is the reference for an athlete to begin a smooth sequence and connect all the dots in a set of movements. The front foot, when it arrives at the finish line, is a great reference point. Teaching from the ground up is nothing new, the same as building from the foundation or ground up.

I have seen Big League Hitting Coaches perform video analysis. And they generally begin the analysis from the moment of the landing of the front foot. Interesting? Yes. So I had to take a closer look at that.

Let's get one thing straight—so many people think computers multitask but they actually do not. A computer handles tasks sequentially—it switches back and forth between more than one process; therefore it is distracted from one thing, while it focuses on something else. A lot like today's youth. ie., text messaging, talking, homework, etc.

Any computer person will tell you that a computer with one processor can only do one thing at a time. Computers have the ability to change tasks very quickly. So, what might appear as multi-tasking really isn't. Computers actually time-slice, meaning they give a few milliseconds to one task, then another, and then another. Computers cannot multi-task and neither can you—yes that's correct—you can't either.

It seems that so many hitters are attempting to *read* and *evaluate* a pitch during the timing phase—which generally happens pre-pitch. In cognitive functions such as hitting, one cannot multi task. If the timing of toe-touch/ heel-plant and tracking/recognition are happening simultaneously, then one of them will not be as fast or accurate. In fact, during the last 15 feet of the flight of the pitch, the brain and eyes cannot work together fast enough, thus making the ball virtually invisible. Thus there is a blind spot where there is virtually no visibility of the ball so the TTC is anticipated—never seen.

I am stating here that when the front foot has completed the task of the toe-touch/heel-plant, it is easier to then focus on the read. Evaluating the pitch simultaneous to the toe-touch/heel-plant distracts hitters from timing the pitch accurately. The significance of the front foot being in the proper position prior to the swing is so important for power and timing. It is something that we all teach as coaches, and we all implement as consistent, strong hitters.

Now the front foot has a unique significance and relationship with the eyes and how we interpret ATC and TTC. The front foot has become for me, the primary reason hitters are late visually or inaccurate in their perception of where the ball is and is actually going. Balance, Control, just plain old control of your body is necessary for consistency and is a byproduct of front foot or front-side stabilization.

CHAPTER 15

THE PROCESS: Formulas, Templates, and Game Plans

*"A .400 hitter is just a .300 hitter with
a half a brain."—Rob Crews*

Hitting is a lot like math. It's about solving problems. We cannot solve problems without having formulas to guide us. Some formulas are obvious or standard, and others are custom or individualized for certain players. One example of formulas is a hitter's ability to prioritize what is primary and what is secondary when committing to a pitch. So we train hitters to adjust from high to low, *out to in*, or fast to slow. Knowing we cannot look for a slow pitch and adjust to a fast pitch realistically. See charts below.

Hitters Counts
- 0-0
- 1-0
- 2-0
- 2-1
- 3-1
- 3-0

So what do these counts have in common? These counts are counts where the hitter is ahead. When you are the hitter, and the count is in your favor, learning to make the strike zone smaller is important. This does, however, require a degree of imagination. Here is where you shrink the zone only to places you want a pitch to be and if it isn't there, you take the pitch.

Pitchers Counts
- 0-1
- 0-2
- 1-2

Gray Pitches
- 3-2
- 2-2

The 3-2 count is tricky. I think what probably matters the most is how you arrived at your 3-2 count. For example, if you are the hitter and you were behind 0-2 and then worked your way up to a 3-2 count, then you now have the advantage.

However, if you are the hitter and you were ahead in the count 3-0 and the pitcher comes back to a 3-2 count, then you could be at a disadvantage.

The 2-2 count is similar to this but different with the bases loaded obviously. What pitcher wants to go 3-2 with the bases loaded? A strike may or may not be coming in this situation.

TYPES OF PITCHERS

Baseball
- Hard/Wild
- Crafty/Lefty
- Lefty Tail
- Curve-Ball Happy

Softball
- Up Down
- Side to Side
- Rise Ball
- Drop Ball
- Screw Ball
- Change up

One of the biggest mistakes immature hitters make is attempting to implement the same approach for every pitcher. Once we learn to put pitchers into categories (see above) it becomes so much easier to develop hitting approaches for specific pitcher-types from game to game. We should probably have a different approach or game plan for every category when applicable. For example, every team should discuss and implement a team approach customized to the pitcher-type. And every hitter should have an idea how they would like to approach various pitcher-types. The results should be recorded and used as a reference to know what is working or not and adjustments should be made accordingly. Are you up in the box or back in the box? Are you on the plate or off? Do you ever change where you start in the batter's box or not? Do you mix up when you first pitch or first strike swing? Why are these adjustments important? Any team that has not considered these factors will never beat great pitching.

Diagonal Coordinates System (RHB)

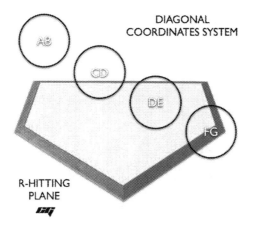

Diagonal Coordinates System (LHB)

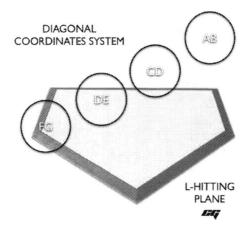

Vertical Coordinates System (RHB)

Vertical Coordinates System

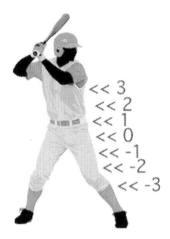

THE PROCESS DRIVEN PERFORMER

*"Hitters will go 0 for 7 on Sunday, and then
Monday morning they will go hit for 2 hours on
the tee. Perfect swing, wrong mindset."*

I asked a Division 1 baseball player what his intention or plan was as he stepped into the batter's box. And he said to me, *"To get a hit."*

I can't stress the importance of the process versus outcome enough. Here is an example of a player who is outcome driven:

*Let's call this player Sam. Sam is a great athlete, clearly
the best player on the team . . . when he is on! There are*

teams who had enough talent to win the championship but didn't. And there are also, players who have enough talent to be great, but aren't. Aside from commitment, work ethic, etc., we must look at in-game mindset. What is your in-game mindset? Are you so concerned with getting the hit or going 4-4 or striking out the batter or throwing the no-hitter? If so, then you are definitely outcome driven. Wrong mindset. Consistent athletes are generally process driven.

Here is an example of the PROCESS-DRIVEN Athlete:

"Okay, I can do this. Relax and breathe. Soft to strong. Stay back and be quick. If I get an inside pitch, fast hands. Here we go."

FROM NOW TO NEXT

"On to the next one."—Jay-Z

I guess the wonderful thing about the games of baseball and softball is that there is always another opportunity. There is always another ground ball, pitch, or plate appearance. We live to play another day. It makes it easy to forget about what happened yesterday when you are looking forward to what is next.

When I am training hitters I focus on getting them to have that short memory. So many hitters get upset during practice, which is a good indication of how they will or won't keep it together in the game. If I can get my hitters to prepare for the next pitch, forgetting about the last pitch, then I am successful in teaching the management of emotions. So I have this two-second rule. A player has exactly two seconds to be upset about the last episode. After the 2 seconds, it's on to the next one. Most young athletes would like to let things go but their parents won't let them. Yes, that was a reality check. Read that again. It is common for players to have already turned the page, and then hours later, get reminded by their parents.

STICK TO THE SCRIPT

The Game

"A bad game plan is better than no game plan at all."

Most people fail for lack of planning—especially a lack of effective planning. That is not only in life but in sports performance as well. As far as hitting is concerned, whenever I ask a hitter the general question, "What's your plan?" a hitter will look at me as though I have two heads. It is my intent as a coach to make sure all my hitters understand that in order to perform at a high level one must master the organizing of their thoughts—a vitally important factor.

When a hitter asks, "What's wrong with my swing," I usually smile on the inside. I am finding that the reason most hitters struggle is not always because they are lacking fundamentals or good swing mechanics. Most of the time it is a matter of pitch selection and lack of approach. Remember that a bad game plan is better the no game plan at all. But having a game plan is a concept that is foreign to most hitters, but very common to consistent hitters—I really have a problem with that. Before a quarterback receives the snap he knows exactly what he wants to do, as does the wide receiver. Before the pitcher throws a pitch, he knows exactly what pitch he is throwing and where he is throwing it. In fact, a pitch doesn't get thrown without this foreknowledge. But why is it that most hitters have no idea what they are doing? No approach. No game plan. Hitters should know what pitch they are looking for and where they want it be. The only thing most hitters concern themselves with is how their swing looks—so superficial. In fact, I have asked this question to some division 1 players. What is your goal, objective, or game plan at the plate? And they look at me as though I am speaking another language. Go ask your team that question next time you see them. Coaches can learn more by asking the right questions of a hitter than watching them swing. Just the mere fact that hitters have a plan really does wonders for them in the confidence department. This is such an under-rated factor. Let's outline the necessary criteria or things to consider for establishing an effective game plan.

1. KNOW THYSELF

"Be a good animal, true to your
instincts."—The White Peacock

First thing hitters do wrong is to mistake the pitcher for their enemy. The fact is, your true enemy is you. Yes your real enemy is YOU. You are usually at war with your SELF; therefore the first principle in the art of war and competition is to know yourself. This is where you make an honest assessment of who you are and what you are truly capable of.

What type of hitter are you? ....
What are your strengths? ....
What are your weaknesses? ....

Take a look at the charts below. There are 16 contact points in a vertical point of view for the strike zone.

Which of the 16 contact points represent your strengths?
Which of the 16 contact points represent your weaknesses?

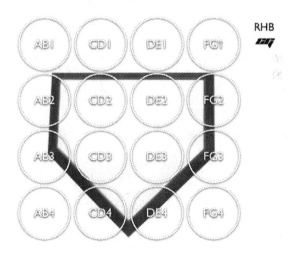

71

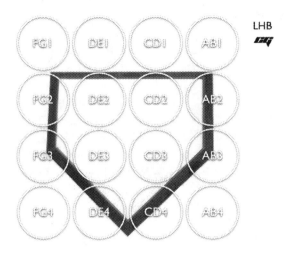

LHB

You have to be really honest here, so that you don't try to be something that you aren't—working against yourself.

For instance, if you know you're one who struggles with the inside pitch, then you just make specific adjustments in where you setup up in the batter's box. Or if you know you are not a good two-strike hitter, then you should be hacking at the first good pitch you see. I never understood hitters who allow themselves to consistently fall behind in the count—especially when you know you are not a good two-strike hitter. Just not smart hitting to me. So knowing yourself and your capabilities are very important to your consistency. The cliché *"Stay within yourself,"* rings true here.

2. KNOW YOUR OPPONENT

Knowing your competition is the next part of establishing a game plan. Here are the questions you need to ask and answer before you step in to the box:

The Seven What's or seven questions a hitter should know before they get into the box:

1. What is her money ball or her best pitch?
2. What pitch does she always throw when she is behind in the count?
3. What pitch does she never throw when she is behind in the count?

4. What pitch does she always throw when she is ahead in the count?
5. What pitch does she never throw when she is ahead in the count?
6. What do I want to look for in this situation?
7. What do I want to adjust to in this situation?

These seven questions are not to clog the thought process or to cause you to over-think but simply a pre-meditated mindset for a smart hitter.

3. BREAKING DOWN FILM & READING THE CARDS

> *"A .300 hitting hitter is only 100 points dumber than*
> *a .400 hitter—not worse. And a .400 hitter is 100*
> *points smarter—not better."—Rob Crews*

I see that not a lot of hitters pay attention to what pitchers are doing pre-game or in game. The few that do pay attention aren't quite sure of what they should be looking for anyway. Not every pitcher is good at playing their hand close to their body. There are so many things hitters can pick up from pitchers—either watching film or simply watching bullpens can help you to determine what is coming or what is not coming. Here are a few ways pitchers tip off hitters.

- Head Position/Tilt
- Facial Expression
- Grunts/Squeals
- Glove Smack
- Arm Slot
- Back Swing
- Glove Position
- Elbow Flexion/Straight
- Wrist Angles
- Stride Direction/Length
- Skin/Tan Lines
- Body Tempo

FUGAZY (Fool's Gold)

Fugazy is defined by answer.com as an Italian-American slang term for something that is not authentic.

Distinguishing between Gold and Fool's Gold is one of the things that make great hitters great. It seems as though young pitchers are taught to throw strikes but when they get to a more competitive level, pitchers make a living on learning how to throw balls when they *want to* and strikes when they *have to.* Having the ability to throw pitches that look like strikes but are really balls is what the average hitter cannot recognize. I like to call those pitches Fool's Gold. It looks so real. It looks so good. It looks like a strike, and then it isn't—it's the perfect illusion. It's Fugazy.

4. KNOW YOUR UMPIRE

"It is what it is. Get over it."

The only bad umpires are the ones who are not consistent. Learn the umpire's strike zone early in the game. Hopefully, he sticks to one zone. This is your responsibility. A strike is whatever the umpire says it is. Adjust to the ump. Getting emotional doesn't make it better for you.

5. STICK TO YOUR STRENGTHS

I feel like one of the worse things a player can do especially in season, is work on their weaknesses. In fact, I almost want to say, "If you have a weakness, try to avoid exposing it." One should be totally focused on what they do well—position yourself to be able to feature your strengths as often as possible.

For example, if you are really good at hitting the inside pitch, you should crowd the plate more. So many hitters continue to position themselves to get outside pitches when they know they aren't very good at hitting them. That's not smart hitting to me. Not good planning.

I encourage you to try this in your games. Coaches, if you can get your less talented players to be smarter, they will realize a lot more success by elevating their mental game.

Effective game plans help with more efficient decision making and helps younger players to grow as the competition gets better and faster.

CHAPTER 16

Thank You

"When the lights come on and the curtain goes up . . . its SHOWTIME. How you gonna dance?"—Rob Crews

I would like to welcome everyone to the next level or to what I am now referring to as the STAGE. The stage is that situation in the game that we daydream about. Three seconds left in the 4th quarter, down by 1 and you've got the ball. Or two outs, bottom of the 8th, down by 1, with runners on second and third. I have found that it's easy to make the big play when your team is up by a lot—or down by a lot. It's also quite easy to perform when it's early in the game—but what about late in the game? What about Nationals? What about the game when you are going up against the best competition? Your perfect swing and your flawless delivery mean nothing in this situation. This is about heart and confidence. This is about focus and composure. This about balls not bats! So whatever your personal *stage* is, a final exam or term paper in school, a presentation or a second interview in corporate America. It's all the same. Whatever the circumstance—you must perform. You gotta get it done. So again, I thank you for reading SWAG 101 and I welcome you to the STAGE.

I often use the *stage in theatre* as a parallel to the *field of play* in sports. In sports the athletes are performing, as in theatre. But the difference in theatre is how they prepare. In Showbiz, the dress rehearsal is just like the actual show. If athletes would prepare at the same tempo and level of intensity as the actual game, then the transition into what the speed of the game requires of us would be seamless. Instead, most athletes train slower, more laid back, and with less intensity. I have even seen hitters holding long conversations while they work on their swings. This is something I simply cannot understand.

The funny thing about the stage is that according to the level of importance of whatever the particular stage, you will see different reactions. For example, a ground ball to an infielder's backhand side during the regular season is different than when it is the post season. What is at stake is what makes the stage perceived to be greater or more difficult. In post season, championship or tournament level competition, what you have done on less significant platforms matters very little. There are certain types of mindsets for the higher stages of performance. Bigger crowd, playing on TV, elimination rounds, last inning, close game, trying to win a position, interviewing for a job, etc.

I remember when I was younger and we used to cash in our soda cans for as many nickels as we could in order to go to the pizza shop to play video games. Most video games would have different levels (or stages). Once you were good enough to pass one stage, there was yet another more challenging and faster than the previous. It took some time to get used to the speed or difficulty of one stage before you could master it and prepare for the next. I find that in sports it is very similar. Athletes have to be able to prepare for the next stage. This is what makes recruiting so easy. College recruiters who are evaluating players for specific stages have to pick the players who have competed at a certain stage. This is why high school stats almost never tell the whole story about what a player can do. This is why talent is never enough but experience at a certain stage prepares you for the next level. I don't know how many people who play on mediocre travel teams have this dream of playing top 20 college sports. Anything is possible, but it is very unlikely if you have not prepared yourself, or been tested to the extent that Championship Level schools will have use for you. A Championship Level school would rather come and see you fail on Broadway rather than hit 4 home runs in a puppet show.

The bottom line is that Big Stage Athletes know how to get into the zone faster and more consistently. Being *"in the zone"* is being somewhere in between REALITY and some VIRTUAL place you can take yourself. In the world of performance, be it the stage, batter's box or pitcher's mound, we actually create another person. And then we learn how to split our personality by re-creating that exact person on command. We actually get into character just as it is done in the world of the Performing Arts. The attributes of this self-created character can become our very own. In this place called "the zone," we are able to manifest a mental perfection that we cannot really articulate. We just do it—instinctively.

STAGE FRIGHT OR PERFORMANCE ANXIETY

"I am a 5 o' clock hitter. I am phenomenal in the batting cage but when I am in between the white lines, I am a failure. I sound good when I am in the shower, but I cannot hold a note in karaoke." This is Stage Fright, a very common phenomenon in performance. Where does Stage Fright originate? And how does one overcome it? Stage Fright, pre-game jitters, or in-game jitters are the manifestation of our fears. Believe it or not, fear isn't real. Our fears are an emotion that comes from our ignorance or not knowing. Fear of the unknown, or fear of an unknown outcome is really quite natural. *I am not sure I can be successful at this particular task or at this particular time—therefore, I am fearful.* In order to learn how to overcome it, keep playing. I learn how to be successful in this situation and when it arises again—I <u>know</u> I can do it. Possessing the knowledge that you can do it, is the opposite of the ignorance or lack of knowledge where fear originates.

DON'T LOOK DOWN: ALTER EGOS AND LIGHT SWITCHES

Those who walk on tight ropes hundreds of feet above the ground, will be the first to tell you—*don't look down.* The second you look down, you're done—and will surely fall. Players who have had consecutive game hit streaks or winning streaks will tell you the same thing—don't look down. Don't read the newspapers or watch the news. Just stay focused—remain in your zone. Continue to do the things that got you there. Do you think the UCONN Women's Basketball team looked down? Gabby Douglass started with a vault, good enough to put her in first place and stayed on top in the 2012 Olympics. She never looked down. If you look down, you will remember how human you are and as athletes we have to be able to come out of our selves and elevate our *Will* above our very own human-ness.

Do you have the ability to come out of yourself? Can you transform into whatever the situation needs you to be? Well the great ones always do. I often encourage my players to create an alter ego or someone other than themselves they can become during the game or that moment in the game. I often refer to this as *"flipping the switch."*

> Jamie Summers—the Bionic Woman
> Clark Kent—Superman
> Bionce Knowles—Sasha Fierce

Dr. Jekyll—Mr. Hyde
Verbal—Keyser Soze

The key to creating and even implementing an alter ego into your game plan is rooted in your ability to imagine. The players with the greatest imaginations are convincing even to themselves that their in-game character is real. *(see play like a betch)* Do you have an imagination? When was the last time you actually pretended? Imagination is definitely a skill. Some players are very good at stepping into the batter's box or onto the pitching mound and transforming into their more aggressive self. Others, who do not have an aggressive self, are way too polite and maintain this good guy approach to competing—hence they are not competitors but participators. This might be okay for golf *(they play against the course not people)*. If I were a swimmer, I would imagine myself as the fastest shark in the water. And if I were into archery, I would become a fierce Native American hunter. Here is where imagination comes into play.

So if you are a nice person, then I am happy that you are a very nice person. But you CANNOT be nice on the field of competition. You must transform. If you do not transform, then you will find yourself consistently under-achieving in the field of play. There must be a game face or a competitive posture. This is something that must be practiced and ultimately mastered. It is also the responsibility of the coach to bring this quality out in certain individuals. Please note that coaches who do not possess the ability themselves cannot transfer that energy to their players—won't happen. The athletes that do not transform have this *"I am the victim"* mindset. They are so right, for they have made themselves the victim.

COMPETITIVE POSTURE

3 Steps to a more Competitive Posture

1. SELECTION
   a. Pick an alter-ego
   b. An alter ego that represents what you lack in your authentic personality but is who you want/need to be in competition
2. PRACTICE
   a. Practice getting into character
   b. The dress rehearsal. Put on your cape. Put on the attributes of your alter ego. Transform.

3. MASTER
    a. Learn to turn it on like a switch
    b. In character on-field
    c. Out of character off-field

"Elite athletes are better at prioritizing what to see and what to disregard. Athletes who are less than elite will tend to regard the irrelevant parts of the stimuli and become distracted by the very thing they were focused on. This oxymoron results in slow reaction times from otherwise fast bodies. This book is mainly about perfecting those parts of the game that are virtually invisible, so that what we SEE is true SWAG."